DITCH OVERTHINKING

POWERFUL TOOLS YOU MUST USE TO GET OUT OF YOUR HEAD, RELIEVE STRESS, AND LIVE IN THE PRESENT

WILLIAM ANDERSON

TABLE OF CONTENTS

INTRODUCTION

Let's be honest; sometimes, when life throws lemons at us, our first thought isn't "making lemonade." Instead, we think about everything that happened, should have happened, and might happen to bring those citrusy situations into our lives. Overthinking, in all its entirety, creeps up on us in the simplest of situations, which contributes to stress, pressures, and the struggles of making it through a day without a headache.

Perhaps you thought it was just "who you are," and you'll never escape the claws of overthinking. Maybe you thought overthinking makes you more productive, and it isn't the cause of your daily burnout. But is it really that harmless? I think not.

In this book, I'll share with you a complete guide to beating and ditching overthinking, by dissecting the very concept piece by piece.

You'll find the ultimate solutions and strategies that will lead you on the ideal path to a clearer and stress-free mind. You'll discover not just the science behind the concepts, but also tactics and practical guidance that you can easily employ in your everyday routines to dominate your focus and eliminate overthinking in a fun and interactive way.

With evidence from credible sources and compact information and tools from research, this book is designed to not only open your eyes to the backbone of overthinking, stress, and negative emotions but assert confidence and assurance to every bit of information, story, and advice shared in this book.

The following 10 chapters will provide you with a keen understanding of the way our thoughts work, and how the different viewpoints on the way you think can create a significant shift in your life. The first two chapters will provide an overview of overthinking, how our mind operates, and the negative effects of such a habit on our lives.

The following four chapters will then provide strategies, tactics, and techniques in both an interactive and demonstrative manner, to maximize each benefit and strategy listed and explained, and to assure substantial results in the end. The final four chapters will dive into special tools of the mind that will sharpen the skills you have learned in the previous chapters, leaving you with an ultimate roadmap to your lighter and brighter mind and life.

Essentially, the goal is to help you declutter your mind, embrace positivity and growth, and equip you with the skills of making wonderful lemonade whenever you get a handful of life's lemons.

In the end, we are the only people in charge of our minds and our lives. Make the choice today to get on the road of eliminating overthinking from your life for a better tomorrow. Today is the day to make a change, and it all starts with this book.

So, sit back, relax, get yourself a cup of *real* lemonade, and take a trip on your personal guide to living a freer, more gratifying life.

1

WHAT DO YOU NEED TO KNOW ABOUT OVERTHINKING?

When you're confronted with an important decision, such as choosing a college, changing careers, getting married, purchasing a car, or starting a family, you undoubtedly give it a lot of thought. This, really, is logical; significant cost or life change calls for careful, proper examination.

However, sometimes, you can realize that your mind is replaying nearly every thought. It's possible that you're obsessing over even little decisions and pondering on the "what-ifs," to the point where you're paralyzed by inactivity. This is what experts refer to as overthinking.

As simple as it may sound, overthinking is exactly what it means: thinking too much.

Take a certain person called Pam, for example. Pam is usually productive and has excellent time management skills. However, recently, Pam's goldfish died, and this led her mind into a constant state of thinking about every bad or unexpected possibility that could or might happen in her life until she developed a habit of overthinking just about everything.

Overthinking doesn't always have to be triggered by something bad; the habit can be developed by or for anything. It's common to occasionally become overly "in your head." However, persistent overthinking might begin to interfere with other elements of your daily life, such as sleep, career, relationships, wellness, or other activities.

Overthinking is a difficult habit to break. You can even try to convince yourself that debating a problem for a very long time is the secret to coming up with the greatest solution. But that's not typically the case.

In actuality, the more you ponder something, the less energy and time you have to act in a useful way. Additionally, it can be draining to continually second-guess your choices, consider all the factors you might have done better, and imagine the worst-case scenarios.

In this chapter, you'll discover the very essence of what overthinking is, and some of the causes of excessive thinking. We will examine the various types of overthinking, its consequences on relationships and mental health, as well as indicators to identify overthinking in your life.

THE ESSENCE OF OVERTHINKING

Have you ever been in a situation where you had a big project or presentation due, and you simply had no idea if or how you'd pull it off? Or maybe you've had a date with the person you think is "the one," yet you have no idea what you'll do or say when you indeed get there. This might lead your mind into a spiral of excessive thoughts, even if you ended up doing great on the presentation, and had a great time on your date. But in situations like these, overthinking has a way of creeping in, and, if we're not careful, can become a habit and take over our lives.

Overthinking, by way of definition, is the practice of thinking about a subject or circumstance repeatedly and in depth. You might struggle to get your thoughts to concentrate on anything else when you overthink or push other important thoughts from your head, as a single thought or situation consumes your mind. Sounds familiar?

Contrary to popular belief, overthinking is not useful because it requires considering a situation from almost all angles and projecting what might happen in the future. According to research from the *Journal of Abnormal Psychology* published in 2013, overthinking is even linked to depressive, anxious, and post-traumatic stress disorder (PTSD) symptoms (Susman, 2022).

Overthinking can make you feel "stuck" or prevent you from moving forward at all. Still, it is not the same as feeling anxious or disturbed about a certain situation. Being preoccupied with a stressful circumstance in the short term may lead you to take action against that situation. For instance, being anxious before a crucial job presentation can motivate you to perform quickly and ensure you are on time. But, overthinking might leave you paralyzed and unable to do anything at all.

Everybody occasionally overthinks. It becomes unhealthy when it hinders you from acting or meddles with your daily life and well-being. Yet, you can take action in your life by learning how to stop overthinking.

TYPES OF OVERTHINKING

There are nine different varieties of overthinking, which, as you'll see below, means that it can genuinely harm you in practically every aspect of your life rather than being a confined issue that just impacts people in a limited way. This helps you to more closely see where your overthinking stems from, which, in turn, will help you to find the optimal solution.

WORRYING ABOUT THE FUTURE

In this state, you are constantly anxious and fearful that something "bad" will occur, such as failing an exam at school, having a problem on your first day at the job, or covering the cost of college for yourself or your kids in the next 10 years.

OBSESSING ABOUT THE PAST

This can entail repeatedly thinking about a past slip-up or mistake you made or repeatedly playing over an instance when you were hurt or in a bad state.

MIND READING

We are all humans and, sometimes, we tend to guess what others are thinking about us. But when it becomes harmful, that is, it hurts your self-confidence and induces anxiety and negative emotions, you might want to take a step back and recognize that this is a type of overthinking.

Imagine you're at a new year's party and, because you aren't talking very much, thinking constantly, *Does everyone think I'm a loser? Am I always a loser in their eyes? Everyone must think I'm a loser, I bet!*

Though we might not get any mind-reading superpowers anytime soon to know what others are really thinking about us, it's important to keep negativity out of your mind, even if you think someone is thinking something bad about you.

OVERTHINKING ABOUT THE "BIG PICTURE"

This refers to dwelling too much on life's "important things," or your life's purpose. These can include thoughts like, *Who am I? What am I here for? What kind of relationship am I in?*

Of course, there are occasions when thinking about these things can be beneficial, but when it becomes "uncontrollable" and "excessive" (i.e., when it becomes overthinking), it no longer serves any useful purpose and, instead, makes you feel confused, overwhelmed, and scared.

HOPELESSNESS

When this happens, your mind goes into overdrive and starts thinking negative thoughts, especially about a current situation.

For instance, being ill may cause you to think excessive and obsessive thoughts like, *I'll never get better*.

ALL-OR-NOTHING APPROACH

This kind of overthinking entails only perceiving things as either black or white. You can examine an event solely in terms of it being a complete success or a total failure, rather than considering both the positive and negative aspects.

Say, for example, you aspire to be a straight-A student. All-or-nothing overthinking might have you saying things like, "If I don't always get an A, I am a failure." This, of course, isn't true. But there is no gray in all-or-nothing overthinking. The black (always getting an A) in your mind is the result of the white (not being a failure). There is no room to be "gray." In this instance, using a B+ as a lesson to do better on the next test.

CATASTROPHIZING

This occurs when a minor issue arises, and your imagination immediately starts to lay out all the catastrophes that will follow.

On your morning jog, the bottom of your running shoes may fall off, and all you can think about is how everyone who sees you will think you don't have good running shoes, or how someone will snap a picture and make you a meme on the internet. Or, how you can never run that route again due to embarrassment. In truth, perhaps no one even noticed your missing shoe bottom on your way home.

MENTAL BABBLING

This is when your thoughts are just nonstop and you are unable to calm them down, even though they are relatively unimportant. Have you ever tried to go to sleep, but your mind just won't "shut off?" This might be a sign of mental babbling associated with overthinking.

It might look something like this: "I have a big day tomorrow. My family is coming to town and I have barely planned anything. They're going to be disappointed that I still haven't fixed the crack in the wall, or got that promotion at work." This is the main issue, but it might go deeper into stuff like this: "The weeds on my tree are climbing higher, and the cat keeps getting stuck in it. I wonder if they'll notice that my window hasn't been cleaned in a few weeks. And what if I bought food that my baby cousin is allergic to? And... wait, did I clean the toilet?"

See where this is heading? Your mind doesn't stop working, and it finds the most inconvenient things to think about. If you find yourself having similar thought patterns, it is most likely a sign of mental babbling.

INDECISIVENESS

You might tend to become bogged down by relatively simple choices, such as what to eat or wear. Making a decision when you tend to overthink causes your mind to go into overdrive since you can't help but consider all of the potential, but highly unlikely, effects of your choice.

For instance, "What will my friends think if I decide to wear the red dress rather than the blue one? How will it affect their perception of me? What if I become a "lady in red" stigma and attack unwanted attention to myself?" and the list goes on. When, in truth, the red dress is perfect, but overthinking will make you think otherwise.

THOUGHTS OF WORTHLESSNESS

With this type of overthinking, your mind goes into overdrive and starts to obsess over *you*.

You might find yourself saying, "I'm stupid, I'm worthless, I'm an IDIOT!" which, by the way, is not healthy or positive. If you have these thoughts constantly, take action immediately to overcome them.

OVERTHINKING VERSUS PROBLEM-SOLVING

Having good problem-solving abilities can be very beneficial. It's easy to think that all of your worrying and overanalyzing is actually solving problems. But there's a keen distinction.

Problem-solving is essentially coming up with potential solutions for issues, which is a healthy coping mechanism. On the other hand, when you overthink a problem, you tend to ruminate—repeatedly thinking about the issue. With overthinking, there is no actual solution. When you get stuck in this thought cycle, you find yourself going in a loop, with no real end. In some circumstances, you might even experience increased anxiety and worry.

Imagine an impending storm. Here are two scenarios that show the distinct difference between overthinking and problem-solving.

- **Overthinking:** "I wish the storm won't make it. It will be terrible. If it does come, I hope the house will be okay. Why must I always experience these things? This is too much for me."

- **Problem-solving:** "I'll go outside and gather up everything that could blow away. To stop flooding, I'll place sandbags against the doors. I'll go to the store to get plywood if it rains a lot so I can board up the windows, and get extra batteries for the radio so I can follow the updates on the storm."

Notice the difference? It's okay to worry about something as dangerous as a storm but identify the distinction between crippling, useless thoughts and actually coming up with a solution for these issues.

The relief and fulfillment you seek won't come from dwelling on a problem for fifteen minutes or two hours. Therefore, try to recognize when you're overthinking and divert your attention until you're prepared to approach the issue in a useful way.

OVERTHINKING VERSUS REFLECTING

When you overthink, you may convince yourself that you are moving forward, solving problems, or, otherwise, bettering your life. However, this is not the case. You'll certainly come to the wrong conclusions and make poor decisions if you overthink a situation. When your mind starts overworking, it generates so many options, possibilities, and outcomes that you become immobile. You will make a lot of mistakes because you have problems thinking clearly.

Reflecting, on the other hand, is different. When you overthink, you focus on the negatives that are out of your control. However, reflecting involves analyzing a situation to determine what you can change going forward. Let's look at a scenario of a presentation that didn't go as planned, and identify the difference between overthinking and reflecting.

- **Overthinking:** "Why didn't I remember to double-check the numbers? Why do I have to be so foolish? This was my first presentation at work, and I messed it up big time. Why can't I do anything right?"

- **Reflecting:** "The presentation didn't go as planned today, and even though it's my fault for not double-checking, I'll do better next time. I'll ask the more experienced employees for advice, and take note of the things I did wrong this time around."

Notice the approach in each scenario and the pattern of thinking. Being reflective shouldn't be destructive. The entire point of reflecting is identifying strengths and weaknesses, so you can come back better the next time.

CAUSES OF OVERTHINKING

As we know, overthinking is a problem for people of all ages, genders, and personality types. It can creep up on you in numerous ways and present itself as something that it's not, like problem-solving. But why does this happen? What even causes overthinking in the first place?

Below are a few causes of overthinking, which can further help you to identify the root of your over-obsessive thoughts.

BEING BOTHERED BY REPETITIVE THOUGHTS

Ruminating or continually talking about the same topics isn't productive. But when you overthink something, you could catch yourself mentally reliving a discussion or constantly visualizing negative outcomes.

FEAR OF CONFLICT

Most people don't particularly relish conflict. Therefore, it makes sense that we want to avoid it whenever we can. The issue with always avoiding conflict is that, like any fear, you're believing that it's always harmful.

Not all spiders should be feared just because a few of them are poisonous. However, spiders start to believe this is true the more you treat them that way.

In the same way, we become increasingly terrified of conflict the more we irrationally avoid it. You'll waste a lot of time and brain power every day trying to find out how to avoid even the smallest amounts of conflict if you perceive all conflict as dangerous. You'll also need to engage in a lot of mental gymnastics to come up with justifications for it once you do manage to avoid it.

Excessive fear of conflict causes a great deal of pointless thought.

Certain conflicts should be avoided at all costs. However, if you allow yourself the chance to practice, most of it could really be managed successfully and with the least amount of stress.

YOUR MIND WON'T TURN OFF

Overthinking might make you feel as though your mind won't turn off. When you try to fall asleep, your brain may even seem to be working overtime as it replays scenarios.

Having trouble falling asleep could lead to additional worrying thoughts. For instance, if you don't fall asleep immediately, you can anticipate being exhausted the next day. You may have anxiety as a result, which could make it much harder for you to fall asleep.

CHILDHOOD LEARNING

The majority of persons who have a serious overthinking tendency picked up the behavior early in life, frequently as children according to research (NickWignall, 2021). And most of the time, people developed it as a result of having no other means of coping with frightening or challenging situations at the time.

A child of an alcoholic parent, for instance, might have an intense fear about what would happen if his father returned home drunk, which may have kept him safe or out of harm's way.

The issue, however, is that overthinking frequently has different underlying causes at first and later on. So, while it's critical to understand the historical causes of your overthinking behavior if you wish to ditch overthinking, you also need to understand the current causes as well.

THE APPEARANCE OF CONTROL

Humans tend to struggle with helplessness more than with any other painful feeling. We simply hate being powerless. We overthink situations because it makes us feel like we have some level of control and prevents us from feeling helpless.

Unfortunately, the consequences, in the long run, are rarely justifiable. Chronic anxiety, low self-esteem and overwhelm can be brought on by persistent concern and overthinking.

PERFECTIONISM

The thing about perfectionism is that the goal isn't about *being* perfect, but about *feeling* perfect. Those who battle with perfectionism find it difficult to let go of things because they don't feel they are perfect.

Nobody truly holds the notion that they must be perfect, which is obviously unattainable. But they have a very, very low threshold for accepting feelings of imperfection in various situations. And the outcome? Overthinking.

Overthinking then becomes a habit for perfectionists as a diversion from having to accept that their work or situation isn't perfect. If you persuade yourself that there is more that needs to be done, then there is also more that needs to be considered.

If you have a perfectionism issue, there's a significant likelihood that your emotional intolerance issue is the cause of your overthinking. To be able to move on with life no matter how you feel, practice enduring the feeling of inadequacy.

SECONDARY BENEFIT

Some people develop the bad habit of overthinking because it has unintended or hidden advantages.

For instance, overthinking can be used as a justification for delaying or avoiding making decisions: if you tell yourself that you can't decide because you haven't given it enough consideration, then you can never be held accountable for a poor choice.

If you find yourself overthinking a situation, you're likely benefiting from it. It can be a hard notion to accept, but understanding the true nature of that reason is the first step in changing them.

MAKING HARD DECISIONS

Making difficult decisions, such as life-changing choices like what college to go to, can cause overthinking. This, in turn, can cause your mind to stress, and lead to overthinking every simple thing, from what to eat to what shoes to wear. You're probably wasting a great deal of time looking for opinions and investigating your options when, in the end, those minor decisions might not be that important to your college choice.

THE FUTURE OR A DECISION IS UNCLEAR

Uncertainty is something that humans simply cannot handle. Generally speaking, we enjoy having faith in how events will play out, especially when there is a lot at stake. In reality, we frequently turn to denial in an effort to avoid feeling uncertain and pretend that things are more predictable than they actually are because we're so anxious to avoid feeling uncertain.

Not knowing what will happen can be scary, and can lead to overthinking. But then again, isn't that every second of our lives? Still, no one likes to be unsure about a situation or their life, in general, and when you are faced with those blurry images of the future, your mind can go into overdrive, coming up with possible solutions or situations.

7 INDICATORS OF OVERTHINKING

Understanding the types and causes of overthinking can help you understand even more if you have an issue with overthinking. However, here are a few indicators you may check for if you're unsure whether you're overthinking a certain circumstance.

1. YOU CAN'T FOCUS ON ANYTHING ELSE

Undoubtedly, thinking too much will consume you and swallow every aspect of your mind. Being unable to focus on anything else means you spend a lot of time considering every possibility and going over each choice numerous times. When you feel as though there is no more mental room for thought, you are overthinking.

Say, for instance, it's been a while since you watched your favorite movie. So, after a long day on a warm Saturday night, you have finally gotten the chance to watch it. However, all you can think about is the interview you have in two weeks.

It might be that you are anxious, but you're definitely overthinking if every space of time and thought is consumed by your interview.

2. YOU HAVE TROUBLE SLEEPING AT NIGHT

Everyone has had those nights where they just can't seem to turn their minds off, am I right? No matter what you try, how much warm milk you drink, or how many whale sounds and nature audios you listen to, you simply can't catch a wink of sleep.

However, your inability to sleep is probably being impacted by an overthinking cycle. According to research, poor sleep can make us anxious, which encourages much more overthinking, leaving you in a vicious cycle of sleepless nights (Boyer, 2021).

3. YOU START QUESTIONING YOUR ABILITIES IN OTHER AREAS OF LIFE

If you find yourself doubting that you can make decisions for other situations in your life because you're having a hard time on a certain task, this can be a sign of overthinking.

For example, you get a bad grade in a class that would undoubtedly make everyone laugh. This, in turn, leads you to start thinking that you're not good at anything, or that you won't even finish the school year. In the end, you may end up thinking that you are bad at everything, or that you will never be successful. You are undoubtedly overthinking.

Be kind to yourself if you're doubting your abilities and finding it difficult to make choices. Keep in mind that just because you're going through a difficult time in one aspect of your life doesn't mean you can't make decisions in other areas.

4. YOU'RE MENTALLY WORN OUT

Consider a scenario where you're thinking about your next big exam. You think about the day, how much studying you have to do, the content and chapters you'll need, and the tools you have to buy to complete the exam. Before you know it, you've spent so much time stressing about a single two-hour paper, that you're now mentally exhausted from thinking things through so thoroughly.

When you start to feel mentally and emotionally spent, you are overthinking. You can experience burnout, exhaustion, and a lack of energy to engage in your favorite activities. When you are overthinking, it can feel like you are stuck in the mud and your wheels simply keep spinning. The feeling of having a myriad of options might be absolutely overwhelming rather than being a wonderful thing.

5. YOU CONSTANTLY RELIVE A CIRCUMSTANCE OR EXPERIENCE

An indication of overthinking is if you continually reflect on past events. You might leave a place with the impression that everything went according to plan but later on, you might overthink it and decide it was a dreadful experience.

We've all experienced an embarrassing moment in our lives, that sends us into minutes—probably hours of self-loathing and discomfort over the entire situation. You spend the entire night obsessing over what you could've done better and how you wish you could take it back. Even the next day, you're still thinking about it. This is a sign that you're overthinking.

Additionally, you might also keep thinking about scenarios that haven't even occurred yet. When you have an idea, it often leads to an episode of excessive contemplation and analysis. Before you realize it, your mind is whirling with several new ideas.

6. YOU SEARCH FOR MEANING IN EVERYTHING

Even while it's true that everything happens for a reason, lingering too long on the significance of something is a sign of overthinking. If you focus on how important everything is, you'll feel stressed, anxious, and confused.

You'll continue to reflect on the event and wonder why certain things occurred. Even if there is no way to be certain, you will question why certain things were said or done. This kind of thinking might also make it difficult for you to forget and move on.

For example, on your way home from work, you spot a dead cat in the middle of the road. Although, sadly, the little guy's life was cut short by a vehicle, your mind is still obsessing over how it happened, who was the driver, who saw it, and why they didn't try to help even hours after you've gotten home. Trying to find the meaning and reason in such thoughts can cause mental strain and issues.

7. YOU IMAGINE ALL THE WORST-CASE SCENARIOS

Sometimes, we believe that by considering every conceivable option, we are doing ourselves a favor. You may be an overthinker if you frequently consider the worst-case situation in your day or the first day of school, for instance. This thinking can, sometimes, have such a negative impact on you that you start to believe the worst-case scenario to be the only option. If you do this, you might start to dread every occasion.

Even though the likelihood of the worst-case situation is minimal, if you anticipate the worst, you'll constantly feel nervous. It may also make you give up on things since you believe that nothing will work out.

In the end, it is up to you to accept if you have an overthinking problem, and take the steps to overcome them. It might be difficult to break your negative thought patterns, just like it is with any habit. But you can teach your brain to think differently with regular practice.

2

CONSEQUENCES OF OVERTHINKING

The fact that we humans have greater intelligence than all other creatures is really what has allowed us to advance to this point with all of our innovations, including houses, cars, technology, books, and other things.

But what if you start using your brain rather than the other way around? What happens if your mind keeps squandering your energy on pointless emotions, thoughts, and feelings? Although the term "overthinking" is not intrinsically medical, research has shown that the propensity can have detrimental impacts on our health (Chukwuemeka, 2022).

It's common behavior to overthink sometimes, but when we do, we frequently focus on the bad, go back in time, dwell on terrible memories, or worry about the future. Leaving your negative thinking cycle unchecked could lead to you spinning for a longer period than is beneficial. Your mental, bodily, and emotional well-being may all be seriously harmed by this spiral.

In this chapter, we will examine 10n consequences of overthinking on our overall well-being. This, of course, is not to "scare" you but to open your eyes even more to the true depth that overthinking entails.

JESSICA'S STORY

Life sucked sometimes. This was Jessica's thought every morning when she got up for work. She had an average life as a single mother, with a decent job, good friends, and, if she was lucky, she'd sometimes get a few hours to binge-watch her favorite Netflix TV show on weekends. But that never stopped the stress of having deadlines upon deadlines, missing her daughter's soccer game two times in a row, and living with the constant worry that one day it would all consume her.

Until it did.

Jessica would always find herself lost in her thoughts, thinking of the worst-case scenario in just about every situation of her life until it never stopped. She would spend hours thinking about what her supervisor would say if she missed a deadline, or what would happen if she messed up on the project somehow. She would worry about her errands and duties at home, thinking that she would miss appointments and disappoint herself and her family. And most of all, Jessica's mind would always swirl with thoughts of her daughter being injured at a game, and she wouldn't be there to help or comfort her.

Slowly, she fell into the routine of overthinking, until she started to withdraw from her friends and family members, burying herself in work and her duties. Her social links started to waver until it felt like she didn't have any friends at all. Then, she started to lose sleep. As if being stressed about work wasn't bad enough, Jessica would find herself shuffling, twisting, and turning each night, and would only fall into deep sleep around three in the morning.

This, of course, led to a great case of feeling sad all the time, and developing a serious case of anxiety at work and in her personal life, which also led to a great case of "stress eating." She'd cook dinner for her daughter, but took junk food and snacks to her room every night as she tried to finish her projects.

Jessica's life had taken a drastic turn, especially when, despite all her thinking, she found that she just couldn't do anything anymore. Instead of working on her projects, she spent two hours staring at a blank screen, unable to work.

Her family, especially her daughter, sought answers to Jessica's drastic change in behavior and soon learned that Jessica had tended to overthink everything for the past four months. She even developed mental health issues, and her coworkers and work friends revealed that Jessica's creativity and critical thinking in her projects had dwindled to almost nothing over the past months.

When confronted by her concerned friends, Jessica expressed that overthinking was her way of getting things done and ensuring her life and her daughter's needs were always taken care of.

However, Jessica's best friend, Holly, showed her that she had a serious case of catastrophizing and hopelessness overthinking. Luckily, Jessica acknowledged and understood that this was affecting her negatively, and agreed to adopt some strategies that Holly suggested to help her overcome her habit of overthinking.

10 CONSEQUENCES OF OVERTHINKING

Overthinking is more than simply what goes on in your thoughts, despite the impression that it is. Like Jessica in the story above, it can alter how you feel and interact with the world around you, stopping you from making critical decisions, blocking you from appreciating the current moment, and draining you of the vitality you need to deal with daily challenges.

Plus, thinking patterns that are more harmful than helpful can harm both your mental and physical health, whether you're focusing solely on the past or predicting the worst. Here are some additional, detailed negative effects that overthinking can have on you and your daily life.

1. IT HAS AN IMPACT ON YOUR SOCIAL LIFE

When we spend a significant amount of time thinking about how other people see us, it often leads to social anxiety, which in turn encourages us to avoid situations in which we might have to interact with other people. Consider all of the instances that you have chosen to avoid having a conversation with someone because you believed that they disliked you or would think you to be odd.

If you give too much consideration to what other people will think of you, you run the risk of missing out on a variety of chances, connections, and relationships in your social life. In most cases, the cause of our behavior is not the other person but rather excessive thinking on our part.

2. BEING POTENTIALLY RESPONSIBLE FOR PROBLEMATIC CONDUCT

Is it reasonable to conclude that you ruminate on the errors of your past constantly? If you repeatedly dwell on the things that you need to improve, your risk of developing mental health issues will increase. When you overthink anything, it might be difficult to break out of the endless cycle it creates. It wreaks havoc on your mental equilibrium, and as a consequence, you begin to lose the actual peacefulness that you once had as a result of this.

3. IT DISRUPTS THE NATURAL CHEMICAL EQUILIBRIUM OF YOUR BODY

Rick Hansen, a neuropsychologist with a Ph.D., claims that focusing and dwelling on hypothetically negative ideas on a regular basis makes your brain less able to differentiate between possible discomfort and actual concern that needs to be addressed (Metrinko, 2022). This chemical imbalance can cause damage to the parts of the brain that are responsible for processing feelings, memories, and thoughts.

If the idea of sustaining brain injury gives you the shivers, try not to freak out. Even if it doesn't feel like it at the time, everything you say and think affects your physical self. So, the slightest amount of excessive thought will not result in long-term damage to the brain.

4. IT MAY CAUSE SEVERE DEFICIENCY IN ENERGY

Have you ever wanted to go to bed but been unable to because of the ideas running through your head? Despite the fact that you are physically exhausted, the battles in your head are still going on. In the wee hours of the morning, if you give yourself permission to do so, you may find that you are thinking incessantly about some areas of your life. When you have worried thoughts, your body is unable to find rest, which keeps you awake and attentive since it prevents your body from finding rest.

In addition, receiving poor-quality sleep makes you less active, which can perpetuate a cycle of exhaustion and is harmful to both your mental and physical health. When we obsess over ourselves and let our worries consume us, the hormone cortisol that regulates our stress response is released by our body. Cortisol's steady stream into the body has the potential to wear a person out and lead to burnout in the long run (Chukwuemeka, 2022).

In order for your body to achieve a condition of rest, your heart rate needs to decrease, and the pressure that is being placed on your circulatory system needs to lessen. It's possible that overthinking will irritate you, especially if your thoughts are becoming more agitated as you do it. This can jolt you out of the peaceful state your body needs in order to rest properly.

5. IT MAY CAUSE ANXIETY AND SADNESS IN CERTAIN PEOPLE

Our thoughts are connected to the emotions that we experience like fear, fury, excitement, and contentment. Those that overthink things are, in reality, the most stressed-out people. They frequently entertain in their minds a diverse assortment of alternative scenarios and possibilities. Anxiety is a condition that can be brought on by prolonged exposure to stress.

Being consumed by anxiety about the future makes it difficult to enjoy the here and now. If your anxiety level is too high, you may experience unpleasant feelings along with exhaustion. Because the feelings that it generates are confined within your life, excessive thinking has the undesirable impact of making you exhausted and, on occasion, melancholy. This is because the emotions that it creates are unable to escape.

Moreover, ideas and acts related to suicidal ideation might be brought on by the feelings connected with anxiety and sadness. Alternatively, you could see yourself passing away or being in the midst of your final moments. The unfortunate truth is that some people will carry the emotional scars of their terrible experiences with them for the rest of their lives.

On the other hand, if you allow yourself to dwell for an excessive amount of time on the things that "might have occurred differently," you will be forced into a state of perpetual anxiety or sadness.

6. PARALYSIS

If you give anything too much thought for an extended period, it may be tough to make decisions. You may have found yourself in a scenario in which you are at a loss for what action to take because you are unsure of which option will lead to the most desirable or successful outcome.

Whether it's starting a business, a blog, or even just asking someone out on a date, you can have the inclination to think things through to the point where you never actually get around to doing them. Instead, you are concerned that the person you are going out with might not like you, that your business might fail, and that your blog might become inactive and have no visitors. A lot like in basketball, if you don't take the shot, you won't make it, but if you do take the shot, your chances of making it will improve.

7. YOU HAVE AN INCREASED CHANCE OF SUFFERING FROM MENTAL ILLNESSES

Your risk of developing mental health problems such as anxiety, depression, PTSD, and borderline personality disorder increases when you dwell unduly on your failings, slip-ups, and challenges for an extended period. Your mental health will suffer if you constantly overanalyze, which will then lead to even more constant overthinking, which will fuel yet another vicious cycle.

8. LACK OF CREATIVITY

According to the findings of a study conducted by neurologists at Stanford, research participants were instructed to sketch a variety of images ranging in level of difficulty from simple to difficult while they were attached to brain imaging equipment. The fact that more thought had to go into drawing elaborate pictures was the sole factor that contributed to the difficulty of doing so (Metrinko, 2022).

The truth is that engaging in excessive thought does not foster creative problem-solving. In fact, it might even make things more difficult. It does not even need to have anything to do with drawing. You might decide to pursue a career in accounting, music recording, or writing. When you overthink anything, it might change the way your brain comes up with creative solutions to problems in everything you do.

According to the findings of neuropsychologists, if you repeatedly think about the possibility of negative outcomes, it may make it more difficult for your brain to differentiate between potential stress and actual stress (Metrinko, 2022).

This chemical imbalance has the potential to cause damage to the parts of the brain responsible for emotion, memory, and feeling. Even if excessive overthinking does not cause permanent damage to a person's brain, the body is nonetheless impacted by everything a person does and thinks.

9. IT HINDERS YOUR ABILITY TO THINK CRITICALLY AND ANALYZE SITUATIONS

Do you tend to think too much about things? Those who overthink often believe that going over certain scenarios or challenges in their heads would help them find solutions to such challenges. Yet, in reality, excessive thinking hinders your capacity to solve problems since it compels you to focus on the issue at hand and to envisage outcomes that are highly improbable rather than coming up with a solution to the problem at hand.

10. YOUR APPETITE CHANGED

Even if you don't want to believe it, your eating habits might be impacted by excessive thinking. Have you ever been on your way to obtain food when an unpleasant idea or memory comes to mind, leaving you without an appetite for the food you were about to get? Or, to put it another way, have you ever been under such a great deal of stress about anything that the only thing you could do was eat? Imagine going through it daily because of your habit of constant overthinking. It is possible that you will not feel hungry at all, but it is more likely that you will eat more as a technique of coping with the situation.

Most of the time, food is valued more than only as a necessity and, occasionally, it is considered a delicacy. Snacking, takeout, dessert, and fast food are common ways for us humans to fill two empty areas at once: our stomachs and our sense of fulfillment. On the other hand, if we ponder too much and it brings down our mood, it may decrease our urge to consume food. When you let stressed thoughts take control of your mind, you might even decide to skip meals entirely; nevertheless, doing so is not good for your health.

In contrast, in times of worry or concern, eating comfort foods may help you settle down or divert your focus from overthinking but, ultimately, this is not a helpful way to address the situation. Consuming meals that bring us feelings of comfort regularly and in large quantities can be harmful to your health in every way. Many indulge in this behavior, which is referred to as "stress eating," because they believe it will either amuse them or, at the very least, make them feel better. When we are under a lot of pressure, we frequently decide to eat the things that are both the most delicious and the worst for us. Consuming comfort food is not a healthy way to deal with stressful situations, although it could help you stop overthinking.

Eating excessive amounts of comfort food or not eating at all is harmful to the body and will eventually harm your overall health.

The way you interact with others and carry out tasks can change as a result of overthinking. Your personal life, social life, and professional life can all be greatly impacted. What's more, overthinking could result in mental turmoil. You will need to adjust your viewpoint to overcome this, and you'll have to constantly work to dismiss any thoughts that cause you to feel off-course.

3

WHAT SHOULD I DO TO STOP OVERTHINKING?

When you finally have some quiet time to yourself, you immediately begin to second-guess yourself and wonder if you should have sent the thank-you email or if you misinterpreted your chances of securing the promotion.

Sounds familiar?

We've established that overthinking is a common human behavior that becomes harmful when it becomes excessive. We also know that your chance of developing some mental health issues may actually rise as a result of repetitive thought patterns. So, why should you stop overthinking, and how do you even start?

In this chapter, we will outline the benefits of getting rid of that nasty habit of overthinking, and some strategies to get started.

BENEFITS OF DITCHING OVERTHINKING

Ditching overthinking can help you live a more fulfilling and productive life by allowing you to make better use of your time, energy, and brainpower. Here are six benefits of getting rid of overthinking and having a clearer, less-logged mind.

YOU'LL FIND CONCENTRATION AND DIRECTION

You undoubtedly understand how challenging it may be to move forward with anything if you've ever been lost or directionless in life. Moving toward what you want out of life is simpler when your goals and priorities are clear. Therefore, having a clear mind instead of overthinking all the time helps you to have direction and focus.

For instance, if you have five assignments due at school, but you're always overthinking, you might find that it is harder for you to prioritize and choose a task to complete first. However, having a clear mind will give you the focus and order you need to list your tasks from most critical to least and complete them before the deadline with minimal stress.

HELPS TASK COMPLETION

It's so much simpler to complete tasks when you have a clear understanding of your motivations. If you've ever wished to develop a new habit like exercising every day, only to quit after five days, this could be due to overthinking about your goal too much, which leads to doubt and limiting beliefs.

Say, for instance, you and your friend have decided to start a YouTube channel. You have made your banner, chosen your channel name, and filmed your premiere video. However, a day before your launch date, your mind starts swirling with possibilities and doubts, like what if no one likes your channel, or what if it takes years to get your first thousand subscribers until you withdraw from the idea completely. On the other hand, having a clear mind will help you to stay on task; focused and motivated.

HELPS REDUCE PRIORITIZATION

Have you ever thought so much about something, that you find yourself avoiding the task completely, or finding other things to do except complete your task? We've probably all been victims of the great big P—procrastination. Overthinking goes hand in hand with procrastination. Making decisions that lead you to your desired destination is challenging when your mind is clouded and you are plagued with indecision. Instead of overthinking, mental clarity enables you to make decisions with ease. Additionally, it makes it simpler to prioritize tasks on a lengthy to-do list.

ENABLES YOU TO OVERCOME UNCERTAINTY

It's quite easy to begin doubting yourself when you're disoriented and preoccupied with overthinking. You can see yourself more confident and honest when your mind is clear. A calm and focused mind won't even consider thoughts about what other people could think of you. If you're at a party, for example, you might overthink your outfit, thinking that your peers or coworkers (depending on the nature of the party) are judging your outfit. But if you have a clear mind with no jumbled thoughts, you will have a greater chance of appreciating your outfit, and understanding that you look great.

MAKES YOU FEEL SATISFIED

Even though your life is pretty darn fantastic, have you ever felt bad for not appreciating it more? Instead of overthinking, you can view things as they are when your mind is clear, rather than questioning whether your life is good enough. It helps you become more conscious of the seemingly insignificant things that are often overlooked so you can be happier with the way things are.

When you have an ice cream cone for the first time in months, having a clear mind will help you to appreciate the sweetness and creaminess of the icy treat. If you are overthinking, however, you might find your mind swirling in hundreds of thoughts about how you'll get your next meal, for example, until you realize you didn't even get to taste the ice cream after it's done.

YOUR MENTAL HEALTH IS BETTER

You can better regulate your state of mind when your mind is clear since it makes you more conscious of your thoughts. It's critical to understand that you are not your thoughts whenever you have a bad idea, such as, "Is there something wrong with me?" or "My lack of confidence is killing me."

The most significant turning point in your life is when you realize that you are not your thoughts or feelings, and ditching overthinking helps you to understand this.

We are more inspired to set and strive toward new objectives when we have a clear mind. This mindset makes room for our personal development.

What are some of the objectives you've been hoping to achieve in your professional, academic, and personal life? Clarity of thought will give you more drive to go after them.

STRATEGIES TO HELP STOP OVERTHINKING

Now that we know all there is to know about overthinking, what are some ways that we can get rid of it completely? Below, you will find seven strategies to help you overcome overthinking. It's important to know that this is a process that won't happen overnight. So, approach this next section with patience and determination, and you'll be on your way.

START EACH DAY WITH POSITIVITY

Making the right decisions, finishing significant tasks, and producing your best work all depend on how you start your day. If you have a good morning, you'll probably feel more energized and enthusiastic during the day, which helps you to maintain a clear head and unjumbled thoughts. Here are some techniques to reduce stress and overthinking so you wake up feeling better:

- **Go to bed early:** This can help you avoid rushing to get ready on time, being well rested, unforeseen traffic delays, and the stress that follows. Having a regulated morning might help your mind remain at ease.

- **Keep a full stomach:** Eat a balanced breakfast before heading to work or school. Healthy eating practices can keep you active and make you feel better physically, which can improve your mood and lessen your hectic thoughts.

- **Workout:** You can unwind for the remainder of the day by going for a quick stroll, jogging, or even doing some cleaning in the morning. It might also make it easier for you to keep your attention and thoughts on what you are doing rather than on other things.

- **Watch and read only what you want to:** After you get up in the morning, you can watch a humorous show or movie, or read some fiction rather than reading news articles about a tragedy or other unpleasant issues.

RESOLVE INTERPERSONAL ISSUES WITH CLEAR COMMUNICATION

You may overthink a lot as a result of the individuals in your life. Jumbled, random, or negative thoughts might occupy your mind as a result of how coworkers, friends, or acquaintances interact with you. It is better to approach someone and express your concerns as opposed to wondering what they think of you or why they act the way they do. Practice expressing your feelings and concerns in a way that will allow the other person to either validate or disprove them.

For example, you can encounter a situation at work when your coworkers fail to comment on your ideas during a customer meeting. You can speak with them directly to get further input rather than pondering why some attendees did not react to your suggestions during the meeting. Before they can agree with you in a presentation in front of clients, your coworkers could merely need more information or some convincing. You can possibly find out that they thought your concept was quite interesting and wanted to learn more about it before commenting on it.

PLAN TIME FOR REFLECTION AND RECORD YOUR THOUGHTS IN WRITING

When you're struggling to focus on your task, it's possible that multiple unsettling thoughts will occasionally run through your head at once. You can have mental overload as a result of this, which will make it a little more challenging to concentrate on your current activity. Setting out a set period to think about things can be a fantastic strategy to keep negative thoughts out of your head. By using this technique, you record each worry as it arises. This can be done in a physical notepad or on the notes application of your computer or phone.

Think about solutions to each of the issues you previously listed for roughly 15 minutes each day. You can discuss your ideas and problems during this period and come up with solutions or preventative measures. It could also make your thoughts seem trivial in comparison. Outside of this period, if you catch yourself thinking too much, just keep in mind that you can think about it later. This prevents you from being sidetracked by unfavorable thoughts and gives you time to think about answers to your issues.

AIM TO CONTROL WHAT YOU CAN

Making negative assumptions is a fundamental component of overthinking. You might occasionally worry about events that are out of your control, which can make you feel helpless and passive. Consider acting in a way that can improve the situation rather than giving in to such negative ideas. This gives you peace of mind knowing you have made every effort to make things better.

Assume, for instance, that you want to ask your boss for a few weeks of vacation time but are worried about how they would respond. You can perform to achieve a more favorable response from them rather than expecting their likely reaction. Ask your coworkers how your boss typically responds when you request vacation time. Depending on their experience, they might offer advice. You could design your leave request to get a positive response. Even better, create a backup plan in case something goes wrong.

PRACTICE MINDFULNESS

Thinking about the past or the present while overthinking is another type of overthinking. Considerations such as what may have happened if you had chosen an alternative career path or what might go wrong during the forthcoming presentation might fall under this category. Being mindful implies paying attention to your current surroundings and activities. It works incredibly well at controlling your thoughts and fostering mental calmness.

To discover more mindfulness techniques, download any meditation app to your phone. These can be quite beneficial for controlling your thoughts. Here are a few suggestions to get you started:

- Calm — Sleep, Mediate, Relax

- Headspace: Mindful Meditation

- Balance: Mediation and Sleep

- Meditation Nest

- Present — Guided Meditation

- Meditio: Meditation & Sleep

- Meditopia

- Let's Meditate

Additionally, there are several ways to practice mindfulness, including the following:

- **Deep breathing**: Inhale for four to six seconds, then hold your breath. Next, exhale for four to six seconds, then hold your breath once more. After doing this for at least five minutes, allow your breathing to return to normal. Even though you've heard it a gazillion times, it still works. The next time your mind keeps you up at night, close your eyes and take a few deep breaths. Try doing it this way:

    - Find a cozy spot to sit and relax your shoulders and neck.

- Put one hand across your tummy and the other over your heart.

- Give heed to just how your chest and stomach move while you breathe in and out through your nostrils.

- **Body check:** Concentrate on your entire body, from your head to your toe points, while breathing. Pay attention to any sensations you get and attempt to gradually relax the muscles in each area of your body.

For example, say you've started overthinking about the crazy day you have on Monday, and the weekend seems to be in a race to be over. You can take a few minutes to focus on how your head feels, then your neck and shoulders. You may move them slightly, just to be aware of the feelings in your bones. Then, you focus on your arms, chest, and fingertips, and continue like that until you arrive at your toes. In the end, if you had truly focused on each body part as you traveled down (and back up, if you wanted), you will notice that your thoughts have cleared.

- **Being attentive:** You might start to notice everything around you as your body and mind begin to relax. Use all five of your senses to pay attention to your surroundings: sight, hearing, smell, touch, and tasting.

In this mindful technique, for example, to clear your mind from your exam next week, find something in your room, office, or where you are to look at. Really focus on this object, animal, or picture, and make a mental note of everything you notice about it, including shape, color, texture, and size. Then, you can move on to something you can hear. It might be a bird, traffic outside, a song, or the television downstairs. Simply appreciate everything about the sound, and take note of the pitch, whether it is good or bad, and whether you like it or not.

Do the same with smell, finding a fragrance or odor and concentrating on it, as well as touch, where you will find an object and touch it, or run your fingers through your fluffy cat. Remember to focus only on the sense you are assessing. Finally, you may get a piece of cake, your chilled orange juice from the fridge, or even your least favorite condiment to taste. Focus on how it makes you feel, where on your tongue you taste it the most, and how it slides down your throat. By the end of this technique, your jumbled thoughts just should be nowhere to be found.

- **Standing meditation:** Do breathing meditation while standing with your back straight, feet flat on the ground, and hands in your lap. Start concentrating on your breathing once you become aware of any distracting thoughts.

- **Meditation while walking:** Discover a peaceful area with ample space to wander about comfortably, such as a garden or terrace. Pay attention to your breathing rate, walking style, and rhythm, the amount of pressure you apply to each step, and other small aspects of your walk.

- **Activity time:** Select a task that is unrelated to work and give it your full attention without attempting to multitask. This might be anything from eating or exercising to dancing and painting.

  If you like to read, for example, you can devote an hour to your favorite novel the second your mind gets swamped with unbearable thoughts. While you read, ensure that you focus solely on reading, instead of trying to do the dishes, while having your Kindle leaned against the microwave. Focus solely and completely on reading, and when you're done, your overbearing, excessive thoughts should be gone.

- **Nature hour:** Take a stroll outside, visit a park or a lake, and pay close attention to the surrounding nature. This can make you feel more at ease and keep unimportant thoughts from entering your head. Along the trip, make a list of everything you see and note any sounds or odors that pass by.

- **Thought analysis:** Manage negative thoughts by developing the ability to see them without condoning them. Thank your mind for bringing up this thought and watch as it moves on to the next without you trying to influence or alter anything.

  For example, say you are a detective, and you've been working with a partner for five years. Then, you are slowly swamped by thoughts that claim, *My partner is way better than me at investigating this case. Maybe he'll be sent upstate and I won't.* Instead of indulging this thought or sequence of thoughts, acknowledge it (instead of disregarding it), and then you may dismiss it once you have identified that it is a thought leading to overthinking.

Thank yourself for catching it before it went too far, and replace it with a positive thought like, *We'll finish this case together as a team because we work well together.*

- **Unplug:** Every day, set aside a specific period to turn off your phone or computer and engage in just one activity.

- **Mindfully eat:** Have one of your favorite dishes, and try to enjoy every bite. Pay close attention to how it feels, tastes, and smells in your mouth.

DO SOMETHING KIND FOR ANOTHER PERSON

Trying to lighten someone else's load can assist you in gaining perspective. Consider how you may help someone who is experiencing a difficult moment.

Does your friend who is going through a divorce require some child care for the day? Can you get your sick neighbor's groceries for them?

Negative thoughts can be prevented from taking control by being aware of your ability to improve someone's day. Additionally, it gives you something useful to concentrate on in place of your endless stream of thoughts.

USE COMPASSION FOR YOURSELF AND CELEBRATE YOUR ACCOMPLISHMENTS

Dwelling on past errors prevents you from moving on. Try shifting your attention to self-compassion if you're criticizing yourself for something you did last week.

Here are a few ideas to get you going:

- Write down a worrying thought.

- Pay attention to the feelings and physical reactions that surface.

- Recognize that your current feelings are true and real for you.

- Choose a phrase that speaks to you, such as, "I am enough" or "May I accept myself as I am."

Take a break from overthinking and grab a notebook or your preferred note-taking app on your phone. List five things that went well over the past week, along with your contribution to each.

These don't have to be significant achievements. Perhaps you cleaned out your car this week or stuck to your weekly coffee budget. You might be shocked by how these minor details add up when you see them written down or displayed on a screen.

If it feels useful, return to this list whenever you notice your thoughts getting off track.

4

OVERCOME OVERTHINKING BY MASTERING YOUR EMOTIONS

W e all feel emotions on a daily basis, both good and bad. The range of emotions we experience throughout the day might shift significantly as we try to make our way through the frequently hectic environment of modern living.

We frequently take for granted our capacity to experience emotion and react to it, and hardly ever take time to pause and really pay attention to our feelings. We do not think about the effects holding onto emotions has on our long-term health or how it affects our mental and physical states.

Negative emotions, in particular, can have numerous impacts on our lives and health and are directly and indirectly connected to overthinking. When we have negative emotions like fear, they can make overthinking worse, or even cause it. On the contrary, overthinking in itself can cause these negative emotions.

So, in this chapter, we will delve deeply into emotions, particularly negative ones, exploring their causes, consequences, and potential techniques for improving our wellness.

IDENTIFYING NEGATIVE EMOTIONS

It's critical to understand the difference between an emotion and a feeling. Although there are connections between the two, there is a wider distinction than you might think.

Emotions are considered to be "lower level" reactions because they can lead to a larger dose of feelings. They are first manifested in subcortical regions of the brain, which are in charge of generating biochemical processes that directly affect your physical state.

Our DNA contains codes for emotions, which help humans quickly react to various environmental challenges, similar to our "fight or flight" reaction. Emotional memories are frequently stronger and simpler to recall because of a brain function in the release of neurotransmitters that are crucial for memory.

Therefore, emotions are viewed as coming before feelings, which frequently represent our responses to the various emotions we encounter. Whereas emotions can be more universally experienced by all people, feelings are more subjective and are impacted by our individual experiences and how we interpret the world around us.

For example, let's examine a situation where an elderly woman, named Pam, recently heard that her grandson was in an accident. Pam's first reaction was shock, after which she felt a series of negative emotions, including despair, sadness, and grief. These three emotions, however, lead to Pam's personal feelings that her grandson didn't deserve to be in an accident. She feels as if the family had been wronged somehow, because her grandson was only 19 years old, in his sophomore year of college.

See the difference?

In short, the next stage in how we react to our emotions as an individual is called feeling, which takes place in the neocortical regions of the brain. They can't be measured the way emotions can since they are so unpredictable.

Examples of a few of these negative emotions could be:

- guilt

- emptiness

- frustration

- resentment

- overwhelm

- anger

- helplessness

- fear

- jealousy

- loneliness

- depression

- inadequacy

- failure

- sadness

Have you ever felt any of these negative emotions? When did you feel this emotion, and under what circumstances? When you feel like this, was someone else involved? When did you last experience this? What could you do to alter the situation(s) in which you frequently experience this emotion?

Answering these questions will help you identify and even predict when you are feeling a negative emotion.

RECOGNIZING NEGATIVE EMOTIONS

Negative emotions are entirely normal, as we've already started to examine. We wouldn't be able to appreciate positive ones without them. However, if you see that you frequently lean toward a certain emotion, particularly a negative one, it may be worthwhile to investigate why.

Below are eight prevalent negative emotions, along with their potential causes.

ANXIETY

Anxiety aims to alert us to prospective threats and dangers, much like fear does. It's frequently viewed as a negative feeling because it's believed that having an anxious outlook affects our judgment and limits our capacity to act. However, in truth, those experiencing anxiety are usually more prepared to react and respond to potential dangers.

ANNOYANCE

Do you have a coworker that occasionally speaks too loudly? Do your kids constantly leave their dirty dishes in the sink even when you specifically told them not to? Even though we may love and appreciate our kids and our coworker, these actions might actually irritate us.

Though less strong than rage, annoyance is the outcome of something having happened or someone doing anything you wish they shouldn't be doing. Furthermore, you have no power over it.

ANGER

Has someone ever disregarded your ideas or feelings? What does that feel like to you? Does your body temperature increase, your blood starts to boil, and you figuratively "see red?" Anger is frequently described in this way. Your body is responding to the fact that things aren't going your way in an effort to make things right.

When we're furious, we frequently yell, our faces show it, and we might even throw objects. This is the only approach we can think of to achieve what we want out of a circumstance. If you frequently respond in this way to situations, it's a good idea to figure out why and develop more empowering tactics.

FEAR

Because it is so closely related to our feeling of self-preservation, fear is frequently listed as one of the fundamental emotions. It's an evolved reaction to alert us to risky circumstances, unforeseen difficulties, or failures. Like anxiety, the purpose of fear is to aid us in successfully navigating possible danger, not to make us feel upset.

You can get ready for obstacles in advance by accepting the emotion of fear and learning why it emerges.

SADNESS

You'll likely experience sadness if you miss a deadline, receive a poor grade, or are unsuccessful in landing the job you were hoping for. Sadness occurs when we are not happy with who we are, what we have accomplished, or how those around us are acting. However, sadness may, sometimes, be a positive emotion since it shows us that we are enthusiastic about something. It can also act as a powerful catalyst for transformation.

APATHY

Apathy can be a challenging emotion, similar to guilt. Apathy may be to blame if you've lost interest, motivation, or excitement in activities you once found enjoyable. It can happen when we lose control of a scenario or event, just like rage, but instead of getting upset, we choose to show our discontent in a more passive-aggressive way.

GUILT

Guilt is complicated. This is something we can relate to both in terms of our actions in the past that we wish we could go back to and how our actions affect those around us. Guilt is frequently referred to as a "moral feeling" and can be a powerful motivator for us to improve our ways of living.

DESPAIR

Have you ever made numerous attempts to complete work or reach a goal without success? Did you feel like staying in bed with a big bowl of ice cream and "punching air?" That is despair—a feeling that occurs when we don't achieve the outcomes we seek. Despair serves as a justification for abandoning our aspirations, which is, again, a form of self-preservation.

Actually, feeling down might serve as a helpful reminder to pause and recharge before resuming an exhausting task.

WHAT CONSEQUENCES DO NEGATIVE EMOTIONS HAVE?

While acknowledging that negative emotions are a normal part of life is crucial, giving them too much freedom has drawbacks.

You risk spiraling into rumination if you spend an excessive amount of time thinking about unpleasant emotions and the circumstances that may have contributed to them. You might feel worse and worse about the circumstance and yourself in this downward cycle of negative thinking, which could have a lot of bad repercussions on your mental and physical health.

Rumination (like overthinking) is problematic because it activates your brain's stress response circuit, which results in an unnecessary buildup of the stress hormone cortisol in your body.

Additional research has connected the tendency to ruminate to several unhealthy coping mechanisms, including overeating, smoking, and drinking alcohol, as well as physical health effects like insomnia, high blood pressure, cardiovascular disease, clinical anxiety, and depression (Mead, 2019).

According to a different study from the *Anxiety, Stress and Coping* journal, issued in 2017, those who engaged in prolonged ruminating after a distressing emotional event needed more time to recover from the mental effects of the experience (Mead, 2019).

Also, most people don't realize they're in a ruminating rut and, instead, think they are actively problem-solving. Ruminating can be a challenging habit to break.

HOW MIGHT THEY AFFECT OUR WELL-BEING AND HEALTH?

Our health and wellness are not immediately impacted by negative emotions, but rather by how we respond to and deal with them when we do experience them. Staying stuck in negative emotions can increase cortisol production in our bodies, which impairs our ability to think critically and solve problems proactively. It can also weaken our immune systems, leaving us more vulnerable to other illnesses.

The negative emotion which has been demonstrated to have the largest negative effect on our health and wellness is anger, especially when it is not handled appropriately. Numerous health issues, such as high blood pressure, cardiovascular disease, and digestive difficulties, have been linked in studies to rage (Mead, 2019).

Although this area of study is still in its infancy, it has the potential to provide some light on why we might hold onto negative emotions as well as how they affect our memories of unpleasant events.

HOW TO MANAGE EMOTIONS

Before we go any further, you must accept the fact that these are typical human reactions. It's okay to feel these things. So, be kind to yourself, and don't beat yourself up or feel awful because you have negative emotions.

It's more crucial than you might think to be able to feel and communicate emotions. Emotions play a significant role in your reactions as the response to a specific scenario. When you're in sync with them, you gain access to vital information that facilitates:

- success in decision-making

- everyday interactions

- self-care

Accept accountability for your own emotions. Words have a lot of power, and we can use that power to change how we feel. When we're sad, we need to practice improving—and even transforming—our situation using our words rather than just complaining about it. For instance, you can decide to say, "I'm going to try once more and I will be successful this time," even though you're feeling discouraged.

You'll feel a lot more in control of your situation if you say this as opposed to saying, "I've failed." We must develop this habit, which requires discipline and repetition if we wish to control our emotions with willpower.

Try to pinpoint the origin of your emotions. It could be the person you are around. We will eventually turn into them if we spend all of our time with negative, discouraging, and angry people. Spending a lot of time among people who make us feel bad makes it tough to control our emotions.

Let people in on your emotions by letting them know how bad things are for you.

But beware of "hooks!" Hooks are something that other people do or say to try to control us. They are the tools that others employ to elicit specific responses from us, throw us off balance, and use us in our vulnerability. These hooks typically hit us where they know we are sensitive, making us an easy target.

So, before we get into the details, make a mental note to steer clear of negative people. No matter how close you are, sever that link for your own good. If they are extremely important to you, for example, your spouse or child, take some time to learn how to control your negative emotions (which may also lead to overthinking) and ensure you are strong enough to be the positive influence to bring them out of their own darkness.

Below are some additional techniques to help you regulate negative emotions.

IDENTIFY YOUR EMOTIONS AND EXAMINE HOW YOUR FEELINGS AFFECT YOU

Not all strong feelings are negative.

Our lives are colorful, exciting, and distinctive thanks to emotions. Strong emotions might be an indication that we are living life to the fullest and that we aren't suppressing our natural responses.

When something amazing happens, when something tragic happens, or when you feel like you've missed out, experiencing some emotional overflow from time to time is very normal. So how can you tell when anything is wrong?

Frequently out-of-control emotions may result in:

- a desire to take drugs to control your emotions

- relationship or friendship issues

- difficulty relating to people

- difficulty at work or school

- outbursts of emotion or force

Take the example of going on your first date after months of asking out this person. However, on the night of the date, they stood you up and missed the date you arranged. Instead of allowing your feelings to take over, you send a text saying, "I'd like to see you soon, despite everything. Could we meet this week?"

More than a day later, they, at last, respond: "Can't. Busy."

Suddenly, you're feeling really upset. Without thinking, you fling your phone across the room, tip over your trash can, kick your desk, and end up spraining your toe.

You can identify your emotions, examine how they affect you, and in turn, learn how to regulate them by asking yourself:

- "What am I feeling right now?" (Disappointed, perplexed, and enraged)

- "What has happened to cause me to feel this way?" (My date ignored me and offered no explanation)

- "How do I want to handle these emotions?" (Scream, hurl objects to express my annoyance, and send an offensive message back)

- "Is there a better method for handling them?" (Walk or go for a run outside)

Reframing your thinking can help you change your initial, irrational response by allowing you to take into account potential alternatives.

Before this response becomes a habit, it may take some time. It will get simpler with practice to mentally go through these procedures (and more effectively).

Consider how your unregulated negative emotions are impacting your daily life by taking some time to reflect on them. This will make it simpler to spot issue areas (and track your success).

CHANGE WHAT YOU CAN

You may start addressing the issue after you have a better understanding of your emotions and what is triggering them. You might experience unpleasant feelings less frequently if you reduce or eliminate some of your stress triggers.

You might achieve this in a variety of ways, including:

- reducing work stress, setting boundaries, and getting help

- learning communication techniques to handle relationship conflicts

- changing negative thought patterns

Not all stressors are changeable or eradicable. It's crucial to avoid dwelling on the things you can't change and concentrate on what you can.

RATHER THAN REPRESSION, SEEK REGULATION

If only it was that simple to manage your emotions with a remote control. Just for a moment, consider being able to control your emotions in this manner. You wouldn't want to leave them burning constantly at full capacity, but at the same time, you wouldn't want to completely turn them off.

You hinder yourself from experiencing and conveying feelings when you repress or suppress your emotions. This may occur purposefully (suppression) or unintentionally (repression).

Make sure you aren't merely brushing your feelings aside when you are learning to control your emotions. Finding a middle ground between intense feelings and no emotions at all is necessary for healthy emotional expression.

ACCEPT EVERY EMOTION YOU FEEL

You might try dismissing your feelings to yourself if you're trying to grow better at managing your negative emotions.

It may seem beneficial to tell yourself, "Just calm down," or "It's not that big of an issue, so don't panic," when you start to suffocate after collapsing on the floor, sobbing and shouting when you can't find your cat.

This, however, invalidates your experience.

You can become more accustomed to negative emotions by accepting them as they are. It might seem hard to grasp, but this is beneficial. Gaining more ease with overwhelming emotions enables you to experience them fully without reacting in dramatic, counterproductive ways.

Try this as an example: "I'm angry because I keep forgetting my keys, which causes me to be late. To help me remember to leave them where I found them, I ought to place a dish on the shelf near the door."

A happier life and fewer mental health problems may result from accepting your negative emotions rather than running away from them. Additionally, thinking of emotions as beneficial may result in increased levels of fulfillment.

KEEP AN EMOTIONS DIARY

You can find any disruptive patterns by writing down (or typing up) your feelings and the reactions they cause. You can think about your negative emotions more thoroughly by writing them down.

It also enables you to understand when particular situations, such as workplace difficulties or family disputes, lead to difficult-to-control emotions. It is possible to develop strategies for managing triggers more effectively once they have been identified specifically through writing.

Keep a journal on you at all times, and record any negative feelings or emotions as they arise. Try to keep track of the triggers and your response. If your response wasn't helpful, use your diary to look into more beneficial options going forward.

FIND A DISTRACTION

It's easy to lose our cool when we get upset. However, words said in anger or hurt might only make the situation worse, or bring guilt later on. Instead, when you're feeling a negative emotion, try finding something to occupy your mind until your mind is stable, such as watching a video, listening to a podcast, or playing with a pet. However, be mindful that this shouldn't be your only strategy, and be careful not to let it become a negative habit and affect your communication skills.

UNDERSTAND WHEN TO USE YOUR VOICE

Even negative emotions have their proper times and places. For instance, crying uncontrollably when a loved one passes away is a relatively typical reaction. Or, you might be able to release some of your rage and anxiety after getting dumped by screaming or even hitting your pillow.

Restraint is necessary in other circumstances, though. Screaming at your manager about an unfair disciplinary action won't help, no matter how upset you are. Knowing when to express your emotions and when to hold them for the time being can be learned by being aware of your surroundings and the scenario.

GIVE YOURSELF SOME SPACE

Getting some space from negative emotions can help you make sure you're rationally responding to them. This separation could be actual, like escaping a distressing circumstance, for instance. But you can also put a mental wall up by diverting your attention.

Even while you shouldn't completely suppress or avoid your emotions, it's okay to divert your attention from them until you're in a better frame of mind to deal with them. Make sure you revisit them, though. Beneficial distractions are temporary.

Take a walk, watch a funny video, talk to a loved one, or spend some time with your pet.

TRY MEDITATING

If you currently meditate regularly, it may already be one of your go-to strategies for dealing with negative emotions. Your awareness of all emotions and events can be improved through meditation. When you meditate, you're teaching yourself to be present with those emotions, to observe them without criticizing or trying to suppress them. In addition, it provides additional advantages like improved sleep and relaxation.

You can use any of the strategies discussed in Chapter 3 to practice meditation.

KEEP STRESS UNDER CONTROL

Managing your emotions might be challenging when you're under a lot of stress. In times of intense stress and tension, even those who typically have good emotional control may find it more difficult.

Your emotions can become more controllable by reducing stress or discovering more beneficial ways to manage them.

Stress management is also aided by mindfulness techniques like meditation. Although they cannot eliminate it, they can make it more bearable.

Other constructive methods for managing stress include:

- staying in good health

- making time to laugh and hang out with friends

- spending time in nature and scheduling leisure activities

We will discuss more stress in the following chapter.

SPEAK WITH A THERAPIST

A lot of people don't like the idea of considering therapy due to the stigma attached to it which means you've "gone over the edge." But in truth, therapy can be a great way to help if your negative emotions are sometimes crippling and affecting your daily life drastically. It might be time to look for professional assistance if your feelings of overwhelm persist.

Additionally, certain mental health challenges, such as borderline personality disorder and bipolar disorder, are associated with long-term or continuous emotional distress and mood swings. Emotional instability might also be related to trauma, interpersonal problems, or other underlying difficulties.

An impartial, empathetic therapist can help as you:

- investigate the causes of emotionally dysregulated behavior

- address extreme mood swings

It pays to get help when we need it. In the long run, the cycle of constant negative emotions could induce suicidal thoughts or harmful coping mechanisms like self-harm. Talk to a trustworthy loved one who can help you receive help straight away if you start to consider suicide or have urges to hurt yourself.

5

OVERCOME OVERTHINKING BY ELIMINATING THE STRESS FROM YOUR LIFE

Everyone experiences stress as a reaction to circumstances deemed to be harmful or threatening. Our bodies respond to stress by generating mental and physical reactions.

It's critical to understand that stress is largely influenced by how you feel about a situation. One person may not find a situation to be stressful while another does and vice versa.

Additionally, although stress in and of itself is not a disease, it does raise your risk of developing mental health issues including depression, anxiety, hallucinations, and drug abuse issues if you encounter it regularly.

So, how can we prevent this from happening, and find the best ways to manage stress? In this chapter, we will examine the connection between overthinking and stress as well as some negative effects that it has on our health, where we will in turn view some strategies and techniques to help manage and eliminate stress.

THE CONNECTION BETWEEN STRESS AND OVERTHINKING

Stress is not pressure... yet.

But when you dwell on (ruminate) the past or the future, pressure can turn into stress. This sounds familiar, does it not? The truth is, when you associate bad feelings with those thoughts, you build a habit of overthinking and it becomes even more stressful.

Extreme overthinkers replay previous incidents in their minds and come up with alternate lines of discussion. They also daydream about the future, regret their own decisions of the past, engage in negative self-talk and, ultimately, give in to them.

Overthinkers repeatedly relive events while pondering important issues like, "Why did that happen? Why does that matter?" But sadly, they never come up with any solutions.

Many times, instead of other people or outside events, it is your own reactions to failures, relationships, and everything else that causes stress. Overthinking then becomes a habit if you give it your full attention and make it a part of your everyday life. And the more you do this, the more difficult it is to stop. Overthinking is detrimental and mentally taxing. Your health and general well-being may be quickly jeopardized, also leaving you more prone to stress and despair.

So, essentially, overthinking can cause you to stress, and stress may drive your habit of overthinking, leaving you in a messy cycle.

When overthinking becomes as natural as breathing, and causes secondary issues like stress, you need to address it right away and come up with a solution. Challenge your thoughts if you frequently exaggerate them. By coming up with other explanations for the circumstance, you can create some mental distance and make your negative views less impactful.

Stress is not a given. It's a mental routine that is breakable. You can decide to view things differently over time. If you can learn to control your self-talk—that inner voice that continuously speaks to you all day and even into the night—you can break the habit of overthinking.

Your quality of life might be negatively impacted by mental stress, and the effects of a hyperactive mind might be disastrous. Changing your negative thought patterns can be difficult, but it's not impossible, just like changing any habit. You may teach yourself to interpret things differently with practice, which will ease the stress associated with overthinking.

NEGATIVE EFFECTS OF STRESS

Although everyone is aware that stress is bad for you, not everyone is aware of how stress can harm your physical, mental, emotional, social, and behavioral health. Mild to severe changes can occur in the body as a result of stress. Your body's autonomic nervous system takes control when you're stressed to help your mind and body ward off or defeat the "threat" that initially caused you to stress. When you perceive danger, your muscles tense, your heart rate and breathing quicken, your short-term memory improves, and your body gets ready for the "fight or flight" response.

You can recognize the signs and symptoms of long-term stress to aid in managing it. Typical signs include:

- feeling overpowered

- anxiety and agitation

- feeling dejected and hopeless

- overwhelming fear

- a lack of confidence

- being unable to decide

- disregard for obligations to family and others

- mood changes

- difficulty eating

- changes in sexual desire

- apathetic and unfocused

- social isolation

- excessive drinking

- lower levels of productivity and performance

In certain situations, you may experience stress when:

- you are under pressure or have a threat to your health and have few or no resources to address the issue.

- you lack a structure of assistance in place.

- you go through significant life changes, including losing your job or moving.

- you are always tired.

- you're not in great physical shape.

- you struggle to keep your emotions under control.

Stress is a strong force that can have a variety of negative effects. In small doses, stress can have a mildly positive effect on performance because it helps people focus and perform better in their academic, professional, and athletic endeavors.

Unfortunately, the negative effects of stress exceed the occasional or slight improvements in performance. Many people experience the negative effects of stress on health as their levels of stress rise over time. But being aware is the first step in managing stress. So, here are five negative effects that stress can have on a person.

1. NEGATIVE EFFECTS OF STRESS ON YOUR MENTAL HEALTH

Everyone experiences stress; it can occur at work, at home, when traveling, before a presentation, or almost anywhere else. However, chronic and long-term stress can cause mental illness if not dealt with. The cause of this is that we have a tendency to hang on to stress and are unable to let it go.

The mental effects of stress can include:

- irritation or hostility

- a sense of having less control

- insomnia

- drowsiness or weariness

- sorrow or crying

- having trouble focusing, thinking, or remembering

- a negative attitude or a lack of confidence

- ongoing worry

- decision-making challenges

Additionally, constant stress can result in depression, anxiety, or burnout, among other issues. An exceptionally painful or stressful incident might lead to the onset of PTSD. The individual may continue to have uncontrollable thoughts and violent flashbacks or nightmares long after the trauma has passed. Lastly, poor attention is a component of several mental health conditions, including depression, anxiety, and attention-deficit hyperactivity disorder (ADHD). Stress can also contribute to these conditions.

2. NEGATIVE EFFECTS OF STRESS ON PHYSICAL HEALTH

Even though stress is frequently associated with mental health problems, it has important physical effects on the body. The following are a few physical effects of stress:

- **Body pains:** Your body becomes tense and tight under stress. Over time, this stiffness may result in generalized body-wide muscle soreness.

- **Migraines and headaches:** Stress-related tension in the body can lead to headaches and migraines.

- **Cardiac problems:** High levels of stress raise blood pressure and heart rate. These effects are not troubling in the short term, but they may lead to issues in the long run.

- **Stomach issues:** Stress can result in nausea, vomiting, diarrhea, and general stomach pain.

- **Women's reproductive problems:** Women who are less stressed than others may have less trouble getting pregnant.

Some people may experience all of these symptoms while others may experience only one. In any event, the short-term negative impacts of stress on physical well-being can have a significant negative impact on someone's health.

3. NEGATIVE EFFECTS OF STRESS ON EMOTIONAL WELL-BEING

Stress imposes unwelcome emotional symptoms either directly or indirectly. Stress' effects might exacerbate existing mental symptoms or result in the development of brand-new ones.

When under a lot of stress, people often direct their emotions toward sadness or worry. Without seeking help and taking action, the emotional impacts of stress will eventually develop into a full depression or anxiety illness.

A person with depression may experience extreme sadness that lasts for the majority of the day. Even a TV commercial could cause you to break down in tears if your mood is low and you are easily affected.

In some instances, the worry will intensify into phobias or panic attacks, which are both severe forms of anxiety.

High levels of stress are associated with anxiety and depression, but ongoing stress can also have a variety of negative consequences on emotional health, including the following:

- **Angry and easily irritated:** You could experience rage issues or grow resentful of yourself or other people.

- **Restlessness:** Someone under a lot of pressure could feel impatient or uneasy in their own skin.

4. NEGATIVE EFFECTS OF STRESS ON BEHAVIOR

Stress appears to have an unwelcome effect on every element of life. Since stress has an effect on both physical and mental health, it also alters behavior.

These are some of the behavioral repercussions of stress:

- **Gain or loss of weight**: Stress can induce depression, which may result in weight loss. Stress can also make someone overeat and increase the body's fat storage.

- **Sleep**: Stress tends to affect sleep and energy levels, as well as motivation. People who experience significant levels of stress may discover that they need to nap during the day, exercise less, and feel worn out.

- **Social issues**: People interact differently when they are under a lot of stress. Some people may completely distance themselves from others.

Although the behavioral symptoms of stress can be harmful, there are occasionally even more negative effects associated with coping mechanisms. High-stress individuals frequently use drugs or alcohol as a coping mechanism. Due to this connection, someone may start using drugs or use them more frequently, which could lead to the development of new stressors.

5. NEGATIVE EFFECT OF STRESS ON SOCIAL LIFE

We thrive on performance, competitiveness, and perfection in today's world, which causes stress to rise subtly. Stress is a social phenomenon that needs to be properly assessed since it has damaging effects that are frequently underestimated.

The daily stress we feel is primarily brought on by a number of things that are a part of modern society, such as:

- increased workload to boost productivity
- relentless pursuit of perfection
- compulsion to win
- difficulty juggling work, personal life, and family life
- significant shifts in values and societal standards

Therefore, stress can affect our social life in a number of ways, including:

- pressure to be different or "fit in"
- the urge to withdraw from friends, family or life-long beliefs
- feelings of helplessness, being alone or not good enough
- loss of reliance on loved ones
- lack of productivity at work or school

STRESS'S LONG-TERM EFFECTS ON HEALTH

Stress can have negative short-and long-term impacts, with the latter being significantly more detrimental. The severity and frequency of health-related issues tend to worsen over time. Short-term stress, for instance, might cause cardiovascular problems like elevated heart rate and blood pressure. Over time, the body becomes less resilient and could experience more significant problems like a heart attack or stroke.

A number of more short-term consequences of stress on health progress to riskier long-term repercussions, including:

- becoming obese

- stomach problems that cause irritable bowel syndrome

- indications of mental illness developing into ongoing psychological conditions

Long-term stressed women also express greater anxiety about their menstrual periods. They can experience more severe premenstrual syndrome (PMS) symptoms or irregular, unpredictable cycles. Stress can also lead to problems with sexual health in people of both sexes. High stress can affect sexual attraction such that they have a harder time getting aroused.

BENEFITS OF RELAXATION

Stress management can be greatly aided by relaxation practices. Peace of mind and engaging in a hobby are merely two aspects of relaxation. It is a method that lessens the negative effects of stress on your body and mind. Utilizing relaxation techniques can help you manage daily stress. Additionally, these methods can help with chronic stress or stress connected to different medical issues (such as heart disease) and discomfort.

Learning relaxation techniques can help you, regardless of whether your stress is under or out of control. Simple relaxation methods are easy to learn, may often be used anywhere, are frequently free or inexpensive, and carry no danger.

Relaxation methods may not be a top priority in your life when you are dealing with a lot of obligations and duties or the demands of a sickness. However, that means you can miss out on the advantages of relaxing for your health.

The advantages of using relaxation techniques are numerous. Four such benefits are listed below.

REDUCES BLOOD PRESSURE

The chances of high blood pressure, heart attacks, and other heart conditions might increase due to stress. Chronic high blood pressure or hypertension can cause heart disease, which raises your risk of having a heart attack or stroke. However, relaxing protects your heart while your heart rate slows.

In a 2018 study from the *Journal of Alternative and Complementary Medicine*, relaxation techniques were found to significantly lower blood pressure in people with hypertension after eight weeks of practice (Wright, 2022).

Therefore, relaxation methods could be an alternative course of treatment if you are diagnosed with high blood pressure that is unresponsive to medicines. However, in order to avoid significant problems, it's imperative that you stick to the treatment schedule recommended by your doctor if you have high blood pressure.

REDUCES THE SYMPTOMS OF ANXIETY AND STRESS

Relaxation methods can be beneficial in controlling your symptoms if you have an anxiety disorder.

Experts found that behavioral therapy and relaxation training both help to lessen the symptoms of anxiety. According to the same study, relaxation techniques for treating panic disorders are just as efficient as exposure and behavioral therapy. Other anxiety disorders, such as generalized anxiety disorder, had comparable results. Additionally, another study found that relaxation may be beneficial for patients who experience anxiety following a medical condition such as a stroke (Wright, 2022).

Therefore, relaxation techniques can be greatly effective in treating anxiety and related issues.

PAIN REDUCTION

Relaxation methods could be beneficial for the following:

- **Pain during and following surgery:** Before and after significant medical procedures, using relaxation techniques as part of your treatment plan may help lessen your pain.

- **Headaches:** Relaxation can effectively decrease the frequency of headaches and decrease medication use (Wright, 2022).

- **Lower back ache:** Setting aside time for relaxation and maintaining a calm mind can relieve back pain. There are certain techniques that can be used in this instance.

FEELING REFRESHED

When we are stressed about a long day at work, usually, just a few minutes to unwind can help us to feel better. Just like taking a shower or having a long nice shower or having a glass of water after you've been on a run, relaxation can help you feel refreshed, motivated, and ready to work again.

TECHNIQUES TO RELEASE STRESS

Numerous stress-relieving techniques can be taught by healthcare professionals like mental health practitioners and complementary health specialists. However, you can also teach yourself various relaxation methods.

Redirecting your attention to something calming and becoming more conscious of your body are two general components of relaxation techniques. It doesn't matter which technique you choose, but it's important to make an effort to relax frequently if you want to experience its benefits.

Here are a few different techniques to reduce stress.

1. AUTOGENIC RELAXATION

Autogenic refers to something that originates within you. You can lower stress by using this relaxation technique, which combines body awareness with visual images.

You can mentally repeat phrases or thoughts that can ease stress in your muscles and promote relaxation. For instance, picture a calm environment such as a forest or a meadow by the riverside. Following that, your attention can be directed toward relaxing your breathing, lowering your heart rate, or experiencing other bodily sensations, such as relaxing each arm or leg one at a time.

2. PROGRESSIVELY RELAXING THE MUSCLES

You concentrate on gradually tensing and then releasing each muscle group when using this relaxation technique.

One technique for progressive muscle relaxation involves starting with your toes and gradually moving your way up to your head and shoulders. The ideal setting for doing this is a peaceful, distraction-free environment like your bedroom or private office. Alternately, you might start at your neck and shoulders and work your way down to your toes. Repeat by making your muscles tense for five seconds, then relax for thirty.

3. GUIDED IMAGERY

You could create mental pictures as part of this stress-releasing technique to transport your mind to a tranquil, peaceful location or circumstance. Include as many senses as you can when using imagery, such as smell, sight, sound, and touch.

Say, for instance, you're on the beach. Consider the aroma of seawater, the sound of breaking waves, and the heat of the sun. And the best part? You don't even have to physically be at the beach to use this technique.

Close your eyes, find a peaceful place to relax, take off any tight clothing, and concentrate on your breathing. Try to keep your mind on the here and now and to think positively.

You can access free apps and online recordings of tranquil scenes; just be sure to pick images that you find relaxing and have meaning for you personally. Although guided imagery can support a positive self-image, it can be challenging for people who struggle to conjure up mental images or have intrusive thoughts.

4. BREATH AWARENESS

Take long, calm, deep breaths as you practice this easy, effective technique (also known as abdominal or belly breathing). Breathing helps you gradually detach your mind from bothersome ideas and feelings. Take a few minutes from your desk at work, for instance, to practice this technique. Take one long breath through your nose for seven seconds, hold for eight, then release through your mouth while you count seven again. Repeat until you feel relaxed. It works like a charm.

People with breathing difficulties, such as those who have respiratory conditions or heart failure, may not be able to use this procedure.

5. BODY SCAN

This method combines progressive muscular relaxation with breath awareness. You should focus on one body area or group of muscles at a time after a few minutes of deep breathing, mentally releasing whatever physical tension you may be feeling there. Your perception of the mind-body link may be improved with the help of a body scan.

You may refer to the point "Body check" in Chapter 3 under the *Practice Mindfulness* heading for more information.

This method may be less useful for you if you just underwent surgery that has an impact on your body image or experience other issues with body image.

LEARNING THESE TECHNIQUES REQUIRES PRACTICE

You can become more conscious of muscle tension and other stress-related physical symptoms as you practice relaxation techniques. When you are aware of how the stress response feels, you may deliberately try to relax as soon as you see any signs of stress. By doing this, you can stop stress from getting out of hand.

Always keep in mind that relaxing methods are skills. Your ability to relax becomes better with practice, just like any other skill. So, don't be too hard on yourself. Avoid making your attempts to relax become yet another source of stress. Try a different relaxation method if the first one doesn't work for you.

Remember that some people may experience emotional distress while using various relaxation techniques, particularly those with severe mental health conditions and a history of abuse. So, even though it's uncommon, stop practicing a technique if you start to feel emotional pain. Think about speaking with your doctor or a mental health professional.

6

OVERCOME OVERTHINKING BY MASTERING YOUR TIME

To do more each day, the secret is to arrange your tasks and make efficient use of your time. This may lower stress levels and boost both at-home and professional productivity. It can also help reduce the issue of overthinking, which makes it a key skill to learn in this book. Poor time management can lead to stress, which can then turn into constant overthinking. So, learning how to effectively manage your time against tasks is essential on your road to ditching overthinking.

Each person develops time management abilities differently over time. The key here is figuring out what suits you and your hectic schedule the best.

All you have left are 24 hours at the end of the day. You have to do your work-related responsibilities, study, engage in a hobby, take care of yourself, and enjoy time with your family during this period. Events and noteworthy occasions are entirely different matters.

How does one manage so much in such a little amount of time? Time management is the art of accomplishing this without going insane. So, in this chapter, we will cover the basis of time management: prioritizing and scheduling, to help manage your hectic days, weeks, and months, and reduce the jumbled thoughts in your head.

ESTABLISH PRIORITIES

We all have priorities, whether we choose them purposely or not. We hold and value things or people as more important than others, and that is the very essence of a priority. Consequently, something with a high priority is more significant to us and is, therefore, given more attention or care—at least, that is the intention.

What happens, though, if we are unable to identify our top priorities? What if we're having trouble juggling several competing, high-priority tasks? Or if we're simply too busy to finish the high-priority tasks?

The highest priorities should receive the majority of our time and attention. But before we can achieve that, we need to choose our priorities. What does "high priority" even mean to us?

Depending on which area of our lives we're considering, the answer probably varies. Do we prioritize our jobs, our relationships, our families, or our well-being? In order to establish which are your top priority in each area of your life, let's chat a little bit about how to identify our priorities.

HOW TO IDENTIFY YOUR PRIORITIES

A few years ago, Isaac realized that he was burning out far too frequently. He tried doing a million "important" things at once through multitasking, he didn't know how to choose a task and stick to it, and it was hard for him to manage his time because of this. He understood that he had to stop concentrating on the things he *thought* were important but were actually less urgent than some tasks that he overlooked.

Isaac then changed his attention back to figuring out the kind of life he wanted to have. He was able to determine what matters most to him thanks to this. From there, he was able to identify his priorities—his job, adventures, and things that satisfied his moral principles. He was able to do this by identifying his priorities.

Many of us, like Isaac, feel as though our attention is diverted by urgent matters while our true priorities are ignored. Many people are "reactors." That is, rather than prioritizing things that are essential to them personally, they live their lives in response to the priorities that other people set for them. Many people, whether it's their work or their family, spend the majority of their days responding to emails, calls, invitations, and demands from others.

This, as should be expected, causes unhappiness and even overthinking.

Priorities, on the other hand, provide you the chance to exercise personal choice and act out your values on a daily basis. Therefore, below are five tips for identifying and pursuing your priorities.

DESCRIBE YOUR VALUES

We frequently fall back on the ideals of our family or culture rather than considering our own values. Take some time to reflect on your values, principles, and beliefs.

Avoid focusing on things like money, a promotion, fame, praise, or other people's approval as rewards.

Take stock of the previous six months. Write out your goals for maintaining, enhancing, or changing each area of your life, including relationships, health, finances, work, spirituality, and personal life. After that, go over everything you wrote and come up with specific plans to ensure you take the actions to meet these priorities.

For example, you might make it a priority to connect with old friends, so you decide to set up a coffee date every week. Or, you may decide to spend an entire uninterrupted hour with your partner after work. So, prioritizing quality time with them is important.

APPLY THE "RULE OF THREES"

When we think we can accomplish too much in a day, our priorities frequently get disorganized. To identify your priorities, make a list of everything that you need to do, then group them in lists of threes according to urgency. Take on no more than three tasks daily. Anything you achieve beyond that is just gravy on top!

ANALYZE YOUR WORK SITUATION

You have priorities at work, school, or home. Responding to these questions can help you establish priorities that match both your values and the aim of your career or academic life:

- What brings you here?

- What are your responsibilities and areas of strength?

- Are others depending on you to complete these tasks and responsibilities?

- What do you hope to achieve at the end?

Keeping a list of goals close to hand is important. This helps you to determine if an activity fulfills your obligations or goals.

FOCUS ON WHAT MATTERS

Urgent tasks frequently relate to other people's objectives. On the other hand, important tasks serve your values and longer-term goals. A last-minute invitation to a networking event or browsing social media for inspiration to write your paper are examples of urgent yet irrelevant tasks. However, say, for example, to concentrate on a significant side project, you decline invitations to networking events.

Instead of reacting and losing critical mental energy and concentration needed to work on the "essential" things, the objective is to become more purposeful and protective of your time.

THINK TWICE BEFORE MAKING A DECISION

When you are walking into something, ask yourself:

- How does it align with the goals I'm pursuing?

- Have I got the time and energy to complete this project?

- If I don't have the time or energy to devote to it, what would I need to give up?

You can make a sound decision when you take the time to reflect on yourself.

TYPES OF PRIORITIES

To help you identify your priorities further, we can take a look at the types of priorities that exist. You can then separate them accordingly to help manage your time.

WORK PRIORITIES

By establishing priorities for our job, we may make sure that we complete the most crucial tasks and advance in our careers or into more fulfilling positions. Make a list of the important things you need to complete and prioritize them. Next, rank these tasks according to significance. Make sure to include any information indicating if one activity must follow after another or is reliant upon another.

PRIORITIES IN RELATIONSHIPS

Setting goals for our relationships—whether they be social or romantic—can help us get more out of them. Perhaps there are some individuals we like to see over others. Maybe there are some hobbies that improve our relationships while others simply kind of leave us feeling empty. Or, perhaps there are things we have to do to keep our relationships strong. The bottom line is acknowledging who is more important and the amount of time you wish to spend with them is vital.

FAMILY PRIORITIES

Our families—children, parents, siblings, aunts, uncles, and grandparents—are another crucial priority area. What are the most important steps you need to take to look after these relationships? Depending on the dynamics of your family or the ties you have with particular family members, your response can be very different. So, pause a moment to consider your family's top priorities.

LIFE PRIORITIES

There are other significant areas of life with vital priorities in addition to the realms of life we've just discussed. You might prioritize things like your financial situation, purpose in life, mental or physical health, or personal development. Here is an example of a sample life priorities list:

- keeping a wholesome diet

- regularly exercising

- remaining debt-free

- saving up enough cash to get a house

- pursuing activities that make you happy

- pursuing a goal or mission

- visiting a therapist to address depression or anxiety

- gaining fresh knowledge

WHAT ARE YOUR MAIN CONCERNS?

You may be thinking, *How do I prioritize my priorities?* if you've given your priorities in each of your life domains some thought.

So, take a moment to consider or review your top priorities in each area of your life. Combine these into a single long list of priorities, once more placing the highest priority items at the top. Now, this may not be simple. Even though all of our priorities may appear to be equally vital, try to prioritize in a certain order.

No one else will see your list, so don't be concerned. Try to avoid feeling bad or worrying about what other people may think. Just concentrate on what's most significant to you. But bear in mind that it's okay if your priorities alter over time.

SPECIFY YOUR GOALS

Success depends on persistent hard work, but that labor needs to be planned and directed. When you choose to set your goals, you ensure that your efforts are leading you toward a certain, desired result.

WHAT IS SETTING GOALS?

Setting goals is the process of coming up with practical objectives for your business or yourself. Whether they are team or personal goals, when you set them, you decide what constitutes progress or success. These victories and turning points in development may happen soon or far in the future.

Making quantifiable action plans is important to define goals that are achieved. These make sure you're setting time-bound goals as well as measurable goals. Once you have outlined the procedures to reach your goals and have clearly defined the intended results, your chances of success rise.

Goals can either be short-term, long-term, or life goals:

- **Short-term:** These are smaller goals that can be completed quickly. These are designed to inspire an individual or group to pursue more difficult objectives. Short-term objectives include things like drinking a certain amount of water for a day, decluttering your inbox, or losing a few pounds in six months.

- **Long-term:** These are significant objectives that will take more time and effort to complete. Long-term future goals typically involve more ambitious objectives, hence it is crucial to establish and define these goals. Long-term objectives can include finding employment as a doctor, building your family home, or mastering a foreign language.

- **Life goals:** These take the form of long-term goals, and might consist of short-term goals to make it happen. Life ambitions might range from becoming a successful writer to operating a self-sufficient business to developing a new invention (who knows?!).

USING YOUR PRIORITIES TO ESTABLISH GOALS IN 5 STEPS

Once we have our priorities straight and understand what type of goal we want to set, it becomes much clearer to establish long- or short-term goals. Knowing what is most important and what you are aiming for will then pave the way for you to create the necessary steps in a time-efficient and orderly manner, allowing you to maximize both productivity and benefits.

And this, in the end, will make your life easier, less stressed, and of course, reduce your tendency to constantly be overthinking your goals and properties. So, here are five steps to establish your goals using the priorities you've identified.

BRAINSTORM ACTIONABLE GOALS

Start the process of defining goals by brainstorming ideas. Goal-setting typically begins with a brainstorming process to evaluate and select practical goals that promote self-improvement. For example, perhaps you've made spending time with your family a priority. A goal you might want to make is holding a family trip every summer or winter for an entire weekend.

ESTABLISH ATTAINABLE AND DETAILED OBJECTIVES

Keep your objectives realistic and precise. By adding realistic specifics to your goal statement, such as "For this year's trip, I'll need to save at least a thousand dollars," you may avoid making generalized statements like "save enough money." If you are successful, you will change general goals into precise ones.

ORGANIZE GOALS INTO MANAGEABLE STEPS

You can use clear planning to influence behavior by breaking down big goals into smaller ones. You establish a time-bound goal at each stage to assist you in achieving several targets along the way to a bigger goal. These more manageable goals can be recorded in a notebook. To keep yourself motivated as you make progress, refer back to these journals.

IDENTIFY POTENTIAL BARRIERS

Envision not only new objectives but also potential roadblocks. For instance, if you want to go on your trip this summer, consider all the possible roadblocks like booked-out hotels. This will then help you to plan better and make your goal more attainable.

SET A TIME LIMIT

You may accomplish short- or long-term goals and actionable activities by creating a timetable and faithfully sticking to it. It is much more probable that you will actually plan out each step necessary to accomplish your goals in a fair length of time if you set realistic deadlines.

PRIORITIZING GOALS

Prioritizing your goals means tackling everything on your to-do list while beginning the day with what matters most. Why wouldn't you want to exert the most effort toward the goals that have the potential to yield the benefit? You do, and goal prioritizing can help you locate these goals and plan how to reach them.

Prioritizing goals can reduce stress and increase productivity. Since it enables you to allocate your time among your objectives, it can also enhance your time management abilities.

Let's assume that you've already stated your goals and identified all the resources you'll need to achieve them. Prioritizing goals is a crucial aspect of productivity. The steps listed below will help you incorporate goal prioritization into what you're already doing. This will allow you to schedule very little time for prioritizing your day and selecting critical tasks.

DISSECT EACH AIM

Once your goal has been determined (using the five steps above), you should compile a list of the extremely detailed tasks necessary to achieve them. This will provide you with a clear understanding of the type and volume of labor necessary to achieve your goals. Additionally, establish a general idea of how long each task might take. Afterward, you can order tasks according to when (or, if recurring, how frequently) they need to be finished.

TRACK YOUR DEVELOPMENT

You should continuously monitor your progress as you work toward your goals. By doing this, you can clearly see where you are in the process right now and afterward review everything to better plan your work. You might erase the goals or tasks that are lower on your list if you are obviously falling behind on your existing goals. You are giving your best effort, and that's what counts; therefore, don't feel bad.

HOLD YOURSELF RESPONSIBLE

Although it's a crucial first step, setting and prioritizing goals is only half the battle. As soon as you start working, you'll need to maintain your attention, diligence, and resolve to avoid making a mistake. Here, keeping yourself accountable can be achieved by making a calendar and detailed to-do lists.

REDUCE DISTRACTIONS

Sure, you might not hesitate to check your phone while at work, but even fleeting glimpses divert your attention from your job. If a meeting doesn't have a clear, compelling objective, call it off since even meetings can be distractions. You're probably holding too many meetings if you frequently hear the phrase: "This meeting could've been an email." Drop some in favor of focusing solely on your goals.

You can clearly see where to invest your time, energy, and resources by prioritizing your goals. With the goal-prioritizing techniques mentioned above, you can decide which goals should be prioritized first and even share these strategies with others.

After your list of goals has been tackled, you can produce a wealth of triumphs both now and in the future.

SCHEDULING

A work-life balance can be established and time management skills can be improved by using effective scheduling. Discover various planning strategies to help you organize your day or week and increase productivity.

There are moments when it seems like there are not enough hours in the day. When this occurs, it may be beneficial to consider a day as 24 separate blocks of time rather than as a unified entity. You can set aside specific time for working, socializing, eating, and having personal or family time by segmenting each block.

You won't constantly feel as though your time is running out if you have a clear grasp of how you're spending it. Even on days when you don't feel particularly productive, daily preparation might help you position yourself for success.

After you know what you're aiming for, turn your goals into a micro routine. Make a schedule that should include spending time with your family, working out, and doing the things you love.

FOUR ADVANTAGES OF A SCHEDULE

Maintaining a daily plan helps boost productivity. Take into account the following advantages of scheduling:

- **Maintain appointments:** By setting notifications or noting when important appointments are approaching in your day, you can avoid missing phone calls or meetings.

- **Improve your priorities:** Scheduling helps you to properly manage your priorities by time. So, you'll know how much time it takes to complete a task from most important to least.

- **Stay on course:** Scheduling helps you to avoid procrastination and stay on top of your work. They can aid in planning and ensure that important tasks are completed.

- **Set aside personal time:** It's crucial to keep a balance between work and life. Free time slots are visible when you glance at your schedule. Overcommitting yourself might result in stress and fewer social contacts, so always take a holistic approach to planning or put holds in place for time to unwind, so that you can look after your mental health and engage in joy-inducing activities.

Of course, having a more organized day will reduce the number of things clouding your mind. So, ultimately, one of the best advantages of having a schedule is reducing overthinking.

FOUR EXAMPLES OF USEFUL SCHEDULES

You can plan your time in a variety of ways. However, there are several types of schedule templates that you can consider:

- **Daily schedule:** Use a handwritten list or a digital calendar with things to be accomplished listed in one column and the number of hours in the day in the other. Find a system that works best for you to schedule your day and mark things off as you finish them. You may constantly think ahead and consider what is coming up the following day by using a daily schedule. When scheduling, make sure to provide some free time each day for yourself.

- **Weekly schedule:** A weekly planner can offer you a broad overview of what you want to do on which days of the week without requiring you to schedule your tasks down to the hour. To make this planner as detailed or comprehensive as you can, you may include an ordering of events or the length of time required for particular tasks.

- **Bullet diaries**: Keep a bullet diary to keep your daily agenda simple. The daily tasks are listed in these journals with bullet points. One page might be used each day. List each task and check it off when you do it.

- **Goal prioritizing:** For your artistic or personal work, a strict scheduling tool might not be necessary. You can create a list of the activities and procedures required to achieve your goals in a regular notebook by mapping out your goals. To come up with goals and action items, use this more open, unstructured area. Regularly check in with it to determine if you are on track.

CREATING A SCHEDULE

Consider the following recommendations to improve your time management when you construct a timetable based on your regular activities and responsibilities.

MAKE A TO-DO LIST

Before you can start organizing your to-dos for the day, you should first write down everything that you have to finish for the day on a separate list. Include on your list things like appointments, workouts, and meetings that you have to attend on a regular basis. Add responsibilities that occur less frequently, such as making phone calls or meeting deadlines. You have the option of customizing the level of detail included in your list of things to accomplish.

It is not necessary for you to have a complete understanding of all that needs to be completed throughout the forthcoming week. You are free to add any new responsibilities that arise to the list of things you need to complete at any time.

TAKE NOTICE OF VITAL OBLIGATIONS

In order to get organized, highlight the actions that are the most important. Make a note of which ones require more detailed time-blocking so that you can account for the fact that some will require less time than others.

After establishing which of the jobs you need to perform are the most pressing, you can proceed to compile a list of those tasks in a hierarchical format.

BUILD A TIMELINE

You can use a paper planner, computer programs, or both to organize your work based on the time of day. You might find it helpful to schedule time-consuming tasks or meetings early in the day, giving you the rest of the day to move at a more leisurely pace. After a full night's sleep and breakfast, your levels of energy will be at their highest in the morning; therefore, you should strive to schedule your day in such a way that takes advantage of this fact.

MAKE SURE YOU DON'T GO OFF TRACK

It is simple to stray from your newly established pattern, which makes it simple for undesirable behaviors to take their place. You may remind yourself to check in with your progress and timing by configuring alerts or notifications to be sent to your phone.

MAKE TIME FOR YOUR PERSONAL DEVELOPMENT

It is essential to schedule time for yourself, and you should make doing so a top priority. Spending time by yourself and developing regular routines that bring you joy are essential for lowering stress levels and improving mental health. This can take the form of a morning yoga practice, winding down with a calming podcast at the end of the day while sipping on your go-to smoothie, or anything else that makes you happy.

OBSERVE DUE DATES

If you haven't done so previously, go over your list of things to accomplish and see whether any of them have a deadline attached to them. If you are uncertain about what the deadline should be, choose a deadline that makes sense for the time being; you can always alter it at a later time. In a manner analogous to priorities, deadlines specify which activities are most important as well as the dates by which they need to be finished. Even if you have plenty of time to finish something, there is still a chance that you may forget about it if there are no definitive deadlines.

Keep in mind that deadlines apply to more than just the projects you're working on at work. It is recommended that you establish your own deadlines for personal chores to keep yourself accountable.

BE ADAPTABLE

Now that you have a more complete picture of your daily routine, you are free to begin working on developing it. It is essential to keep your schedule open to change throughout the day and week. The unpredictable nature of life makes it tough to keep up with. Your regularly scheduled meetings on Monday may have to be moved to Wednesday to accommodate new client deadlines.

These shifts will be less stressful for you when you have the option to easily adjust your daily calendar. Because it's a skill, getting better at it could take some time. But, acquiring the ability to adjust to changing circumstances can assist you in keeping your habit of scheduling.

If you are consistently late, you may conclude that keeping a timetable is pointless and ineffective in the long run. Being flexible, on the other hand, demonstrates to you that a schedule is not a guarantee that everything will be completed in the order specified, but rather that it serves only as a guide.

To wrap up, we know that a fantastic method to learn time management and feel more in charge of your life is to create a schedule. You can give your day structure with the correct daily schedule planner while keeping the freedom to adjust it as necessary.

A schedule isn't a prison. Make a schedule so that you have the day you want. Ask yourself, "What's the best possible day I could have tomorrow, practically speaking? What would it look like?" Negotiate with yourself, but don't tyrannize yourself. You want to be productive and have a good life. A schedule can be unbelievably useful.

7

OVERCOME OVERTHINKING BY MASTERING YOUR FOCUS

Almost all of us have been in a situation where we're sitting at a desk with a pressing deadline and an unfocused mind. You might have even found yourself doing just about everything else *except* the task that you need to do. And despite your best attempts, maybe nothing has changed. You may even be inspired to complete it, but you simply can't focus.

In the digital age, we are susceptible to distraction. We feel the need to deal with a growing number of different types of information because it is there everywhere. It occupies a lot of our time and attention. One of the issues this causes is the inability to focus on the task at hand. Everyone wants to learn how to focus more effectively and how to concentrate.

Learning to focus and concentrate can be challenging. Of course, most people are interested in finding out how to focus and concentrate better. But sticking to it? That might be where the problem lies.

Fortunately, in this chapter, we will focus on the best strategies for how to concentrate. We'll explain the science behind paying attention to what is important and keeping your mind fresh. You should find all the information you require, whether you're trying to concentrate on your personal or professional goals.

THE RELATIONSHIP BETWEEN OVERTHINKING AND CONCENTRATION

Concentration is the ability to keep the mind fixed on a certain task, situation, thing, or location. A comfortable mind is equally a concentrated one. You always enter a state of tranquility when you are fully immersed in anything. Because it keeps the mind from drifting aimlessly in all directions, concentration is essential for everything you accomplish in life.

Additionally, work that is done with a concentrated mind is more enjoyable. A person with a focused mind is very effective at all types of jobs.

On the contrary, as we know, overthinking can affect how you perceive things, and how you go about your day-to-day life. If you have multiple thoughts in your head, jumbled and scattered, then concentration is practically impossible. Therefore, poor concentration and overthinking walk hand in hand.

Think about it. Say, for example, John tends to catastrophize everything as a form of overthinking. John's workplace is having a holiday party, and he has been asked to write a short poem on what he appreciates since he has been working. However, John instantly starts to think of all the bad things that can happen in his short performance, until, before he knows it, he is overthinking and can't find the will to concentrate.

Just like John, when we have a habit of overthinking, no matter what form it comes in, it will inevitably affect our focus and concentration.

Furthermore, if you are unable to focus and think about something else while performing the activity at hand, you will make mistakes and take much longer than necessary to finish the task. While you are at work, for instance, you might worry about your health, financial issues, and your family as a result of poor concentration, which can also turn into overthinking.

The maximum level of concentration is when the mind is stable in one thought. If we can achieve this level of focus, we will be able to give any task our complete attention and focus, which will make it simple to succeed. The ability to concentrate naturally results in mental clarity, an enhanced mental state, and a number of other skills, such as discernment, decision-making, and judgment. As a result, if a problem is challenging, even one person with strong concentration can find a solution. If you are overthinking, however, it will be difficult.

When a person is lost in one thought, that concept becomes their world and they ignore everything else.

Many of us believe that because of our hectic schedules, it is impossible to find time to sit down and practice concentration. It's not all that challenging. The secret is to practice whenever we have time, even if only for a little while. Repeatedly doing this will train the mind to stay concentrated, making attention progressively simpler.

This method of developing concentration strength helps us maintain our composure under pressure. Additionally, it avoids wasting mental resources on pointless thought, otherwise known as overthinking.

The bottom line is, difficulty concentrating is both a consequence and a cause of overthinking.

WHAT IS FOCUS?

Focus is the capacity to concentrate on a single concept, object, or subject while blocking out all other irrelevant thoughts, feelings, and sensations.

For the majority of us, this is difficult. To focus means to ignore or exclude all other irrelevant thoughts, ideas, feelings, or sensations. Nevertheless, a focused mind possesses enormous power. It has the capacity for great perception and the capacity to consider the fundamental truth of underlying things more clearly.

THINGS THAT AFFECT CONCENTRATION

On some days, it feels like there are constant attempts to distract us. In actuality, both internal and exterior, or environmental factors influence our focus. Understanding what's currently interfering with focus and memory might help you learn how to improve these skills. Here are a few.

DISTRACTIONS

In the course of doing anything, we are constantly bombarded with new and outdated information. According to research, the mere sight of our phones or devices causes our ability to focus to become impaired because our brains are so wired for this distraction (Usha, 2021).

INADEQUATE REST

Lack of sleep has been linked to decreased focus, slower mental processes, and poorer attention, according to scientists (Usha, 2021). Your capacity to carry out tasks, particularly those that require reasoning or logic, may be negatively impacted as a result. If you are unable to focus on the task at hand, it is doubtful that information will be retained in either your short- or long-term memory. Therefore, adequate rest is essential for focus.

INAPPROPRIATE LEVELS OF EXERCISE

Have you ever noticed how rigorous exercise makes you feel calmer and more energized all day? Even if you haven't noticed this right away, your muscles may tighten up if you don't engage in any physical activity. Your neck, shoulder, and chest could feel tight, and such a continuous, mild discomfort can impair your ability to focus.

EATING PATTERNS

What we eat affects how we feel throughout the day, including how alert and clear our minds are. Memory loss, weariness, and lack of attention are just a few of the symptoms we start to face if we don't give our brains the right nutrition. Because the brain requires specific necessary fatty acids, low-fat diets can impair focus. Also, other restrictive diets may affect focus by depriving the brain of the nutrients it requires or by causing hunger, desires, or physical unwellness in the body, all of which are distracting in and of themselves.

THE ENVIRONMENT

The surroundings can influence your focus depending on what you are doing. Naturally, excessive noise is an issue, but a lot of individuals also have trouble focusing when it is too quiet. The type of noise affects more than the overall quantity of noise; while the overheard conversation of two coworkers may distract, the energetic, anonymous hum of a coffee shop may help.

While soothing music may keep you focused on the activity at hand, your favorite song may quickly have you singing along, delightfully distracted. Additionally, your vision might be harmed by lighting that is either too bright or too dull, and uncomfortable conditions could result from a hot or cold environment. Your ability to focus can be impacted by all of these factors. Fortunately, they can all be addressed.

CONDITIONS RELATED TO FOCUS

If you consistently have trouble focusing your thoughts, there could be a cognitive, medical, mental, behavioral, or environmental factor at play. You may have to briefly accept that your focus is poor and learn a few tips to lessen the effect, depending on the cause, or accept the falls as they happen. Understanding these conditions can help you improve focus and reduce the effect that overthinking has on your ability to do so. Here are four such conditions.

COGNITIVE

If you find that you forget things quickly, this could be a sign that your concentration is suffering. You may have observed that you sometimes have difficulties remembering recent events, that you misplace things frequently, and that you lose your memory at times. If you notice that your mind is overactive and that it is always overthinking about a variety of things as a result of fears or big incidents, this may be another symptom that your cognitive performance is weakened. When things keep popping into your head and demanding your attention, it makes it difficult to concentrate on the task at hand.

PSYCHOLOGICAL

When you're down, in a terrible mood, and all out of sorts, it's difficult to concentrate on anything. When you are grieving the loss of a loved one or experiencing anxiety, it can be difficult to concentrate on a single task, and this can be true even when you are not grieving.

MEDICAL

Diabetes, hormonal imbalances, and low red blood cell counts are all examples of medical conditions that might interfere with our capacity to focus and concentrate. In addition, several pharmaceuticals make people feel drowsy or depressed and severely damage their ability to concentrate.

LIFESTYLE

Exhaustion, hunger, and dehydration are all factors that might interfere with focus. Our memory can be negatively impacted, and our ability to focus and pay attention can be hindered, if we skip too many meals, eat too many fatty foods, or drink too much alcohol.

TECHNIQUES TO IMPROVE FOCUS

Now that we understand focus and factors to consider that might affect it, we can now focus on some techniques to help improve your focus and reduce overthinking as a result. Although there isn't a single method for increasing focus, and no two persons will have the same experience, below are five strategies that can help you get started.

AVOID DISTRACTION, MULTITASKING, AND FOCUSING ON THE PAST

When we are constantly being flooded with information, how can we focus? Ask to be left alone or move to a location where others are less likely to bother you whenever you are trying to focus and get something done, such as a library, a café, or a private room.

You can also close all social media and other apps, turn off notifications, or put your phone or devices on airplane mode and keep it out of sight in a bag or desk drawer. Researchers discovered that having the phone out of sight—as opposed to just being switched off—significantly improved cognitive performance (Chia, 2021). This suggests that even having the phone in sight (even when turned off) can be distracting. You can improve your ability to focus by turning off both internal and external distractions.

Additionally, although we might feel more "productive" when we try to complete several tasks at once, in truth, it promotes a lack of attention, poor concentration, and decreased productivity. Multitasking may be completing multiple activities like responding to emails while listening to a recorded presentation you missed and making phone calls while preparing a report. Such juggling not only impairs your ability to concentrate but also lowers the quality of your job.

Finally, when your thoughts are constantly in the past or the future, it can be difficult to focus. Attempt to let go of the past, even when it is difficult. After acknowledging the impact, your feelings, and your lessons learned, let it go. Similar to this, acknowledge your future worries, take note of how your body is expressing your fear, and then make the decision to let it go.

Therefore, learning to avoid distractions, multitasking, and overthinking the past can help improve your focus.

PRIORITIZE YOUR PHYSICAL HEALTH

Though it might be hard to identify the benefits of maintaining physical health to improve focus, the truth is, it affects you over time.

If your habit of overthinking affects your sleep schedule, having a consistent bedtime routine and schedule, avoiding burnout in the afternoon, drinking plenty of water throughout the day, and using journaling or deep breathing to calm the mind are all approaches to improve sleep. Once you get a good night's rest, your body won't feel drained the entire day, and you will find yourself with a clever mind.

In the same way, simple exercise in the morning can help you get your body moving. Regular exercise produces chemicals important for memory, focus, and mental clarity. Exercise can also increase the levels of the brain chemicals serotonin, dopamine, and norepinephrine, all of which have an impact on attention and focus.

According to the Harvard Men's Health Watch study, comparing those with good physical health to those with poor physical health, cognitive tasks were performed better by people who engage in some type of exercise or sports (Chia, 2021). Exercise helps the body's muscles loosen up and reduce stress.

Lastly, pick foods that sustain energy levels, control blood sugar, and nourish the brain. Foods abundant in fiber, fruits, and vegetables can help maintain stable blood sugar levels. Also, aim to reduce the number of sugary meals and beverages that make your blood sugar levels rise and fall and make you feel lightheaded or sleepy. For effective brain function, your body requires plenty of healthy fats.

Avocados, nuts, berries, and coconut oil are all excellent sources of healthy fats that improve brain function. According to scientific research, fruits like blueberries can improve focus and memory for up to five hours after consumption because they include an enzyme that promotes the blood and oxygen flow to the brain, improving memory as well as our capacity to concentrate and remember new information (Chia, 2021).

Since the body and mind are intertwined, when one is feeling better, the other will as well.

TAKE A BRIEF BREAK BETWEEN TASKS

It may sound contradictory, but focusing on something for a prolonged time can cause your focus to wane. It could get harder and harder for you to focus on the task at hand. According to research, our brains are wired to ignore sources of continuous stimuli (Chia, 2021). Therefore, taking very brief breaks by shifting your attention to anything else can significantly enhance mental concentration.

Take a break when you start to get stuck on a project the next time you are working on it. Change your location, engage in conversation, or do another task. You'll return with a clearer head so that you can maintain your high level of performance.

SET DAILY GOALS AND FOLLOW A SCHEDULE

Determine one priority that you commit to completing and write down your goals for the day, ideally the night before. By completing the important tasks first and delegating the smaller ones for later, you'll be able to focus your mind on what really counts. To avoid feeling overwhelmed, divide big jobs into smaller chunks. Achieving tiny daily goals helps rewire your brain to achieve success.

Additionally, make it a habit to block out time in your calendar to complete a certain task or activity. By utilizing a timer or phone alarm and a schedule, you may teach your brain to focus intensely on a subject. Choose the assignment you want to finish first. Focus on the task at hand for the allotted 20 minutes (or any amount of time you need). When the alarm goes off, take a five-minute rest before tackling the next task.

SET THE SCENE FOR FOCUS

If you can, make a quiet, designated location for work. Desk organizers, noise-resistant headphones, an adjustable monitor, and adjustable lighting can benefit you if you are unable to have an appropriate environment to focus. Make your area as productive and pleasant as you can, keep clutter out of sight, and work to maintain it clean and well-ventilated.

Additionally, you can play some relaxing music to set the environment for work as well. Our brains benefit from music therapy. While certain music may distract you, soft music may improve your ability to concentrate. Most experts concur that while songs with lyrics and actual voices may be distracting, classical music and natural sounds, such as water flowing, are good alternatives for focus (Chia, 2021).

It takes time to develop your concentration; it's not something you can do overnight. Understanding how your ability to focus is influencing your life is the first step in improving it. It's time to stop overthinking and learn how to focus so that you can concentrate on what matters most to you if you are having trouble keeping commitments, getting distracted by unimportant things all the time, or not making progress toward your goals.

Success in your profession and life depends on your ability to focus. You'll discover that by strengthening your focus, you can do more of the things you value while also feeling better about yourself. Making time for joy and happiness is just as important as completing duties if you want to have a fulfilling life.

8

OVERCOME OVERTHINKING BY MASTERING YOUR DECISION-MAKING PROCESS

Making decisions can be challenging, and making wise decisions fast is also not the easiest task in the world. Fortunately, decision-making is a skill, and—like any other—it can be taught. The lack of sufficient perspectives on a problem is the biggest enemy of a good decision.

As a result, many people find it difficult to decide on important life choices like deciding what college to attend or choosing a career. In addition, some people also have difficulty making other kinds of decisions, even something as simple as what to eat for lunch.

Additionally, sometimes we do successfully make decisions, but we have difficulty doing it on time. This may be a general problem or an issue with a particular aspect of our lives, such as finances, interests, or relationships.

It may not be hard to guess that if you can't make decisions, you might find yourself stuck in a rut of overthinking about what to do. Or, coming back full circle, overthinking in and of itself could be the very reason you can't make decisions! So, just like the previous four chapters, overthinking has found a way to become an aspect of a loop in your life.

But there is no need to worry because, in this chapter, we will talk about decision-making, the stings that come with making bad decisions, and strategies and steps to help you make good ones. In order to better understand your thoughts and enhance your decision-making skills, you will first learn about the overall decision-making process before seeing why it can be so difficult to make decisions.

THE ESSENCE OF DECISION-MAKING

Making decisions can be challenging for several reasons, but the primary one is that doing so requires going through a decision-making process that is frequently challenging and complex, especially for someone whose mind can't get a rest. If we struggle with any one phase of this process, the entire process may suffer. As a result, people frequently find it difficult to finish the decision-making process, and even if they do, it's frequently done in a delayed or flawed manner.

Specifically, whether we are conscious of it or not, we normally need to do the following to make excellent decisions:

- **Identify what you want to do:** This entails realizing that we must choose, as well as estimating what the choice will entail.

- **Establish your objectives:** This entails determining our decision-making objectives and the relative importance of each objective to us.

- **Gather knowledge:** This is where we gather the data that will be necessary for us to make a conclusion.

- **Choose an option:** Identifying our options is a necessary step.

- **Consider your alternatives:** This entails weighing the advantages and disadvantages of the various solutions, particularly as they relate to our objectives.

- **Pick your chosen choice:** This entails ranking the advantages and disadvantages of the many possibilities to determine which is best for us.

Additionally, we frequently have to switch back and forth between the many stages of this decision-making process. For instance, we may have to go back and change our goals after receiving knowledge to make them more achievable. Similar to this, we may have to go back and gather additional information before going forward if, after weighing our alternatives, we find that we lack sufficient knowledge to make an informed decision.

Unfortunately, if you are an overthinker, you may not be able to get past the first two steps. After you have identified your goals, for example, you may notice that you are constantly thinking about the alternative ways this might play out, and what will happen if you don't make the right decision.

It's understandable that we frequently struggle to finish the decision-making process or to complete it in a way that is efficient and accurate given how much work we need to perform to make smart decisions. However, decision-making goes hand in hand with a clear and open mind. In order to be able to make sound, confident decisions, having a whirlwind of unnecessary, hectic thoughts is not the ideal condition.

Additionally, making decisions frequently incorporates other elements that make it difficult for us to decide.

This relates to the idea of the fear of missing out (FOMO), which is a state of mind in which people worry that they could pass up lucrative experiences or chances. This is a problem in particular when overthinkers try very hard to make a choice that will allow them to completely avoid regret in the future, even if it isn't possible.

As a result, both cognitively and emotionally, the decision-making process can be difficult. Furthermore, the process of making a decision is mentally taxing in and of itself because it exhausts the cognitive resources we use to exercise self-control, making it even harder for overthinkers to make subsequent decisions, at least until they've had a chance to recover mentally. As a result, the number of decisions we've had to make recently and how difficult those decisions were may make future decisions more challenging.

This, along with the other challenges, results in the act of making a decision being frequently seen as unpleasant, which might lead us to put it off or completely avoid doing it.

Overall, the fundamental reason why making decisions can be challenging, particularly for overthinkers, is that we frequently have to go through a decision-making process that is challenging and complex, and suffering at any stage in it might affect the entire process. The fear of losing out, the desire to avoid regret, and the basic intellectual demands of the decision-making process are just a few of the extra elements that make it tough for overthinkers to make sound decisions.

CONSEQUENCES OF BAD DECISIONS

Sometimes we don't notice, but even a "small" bad decision that we thought wasn't a big deal, turns out to be the biggest deal ever. And though it might not always be this way, it is essential that we practice making sound judgments most, if not all the time to avoid the consequences of bad decisions. When we make poor decisions, there is a significant possibility that there will be negative effects to follow.

Try to picture it this way: Every choice we make creates a rift in the universe. When we make good ones, they fill themselves back into place. But when we make poor ones, they create a ripple effect that comes with somewhat disastrous consequences.

This isn't to scare you or make you believe that every decision has to be perfect, because we know that is impossible. However, we should aim to make sound decisions, so that even if they aren't the most ideal, they won't leave us with a mess of troubles to tackle after.

Poor decisions could be anything like:

- making rash decisions from hurt or spite.

- just "going with the flow" because you are tired or unsure what to do.

- not choosing at all (no choice is still a choice!).

- deciding with the intention of manipulation, blackmail, or hurting yourself or someone else.

These are just a few illustrations. But below are five consequences of poor decisions that can also maintain or worsen overthinking.

THEY CAN AFFECT YOUR RELATIONSHIPS

Some bad decisions significantly affect your relationships negatively. Say, for example, you had a rough day at work, and your cloudy mind, poor mood, and grumpiness led you to take on your coworker's offer of going out for just one drink before going to your son's soccer game. However, that one drink turns into three, and before you know it, you have missed your son's game.

To you, perhaps, it was just one game of plenty for the season, but that might've been the game where he scored his first goal. He would've been devastated that you weren't there to see it, and probably flunk his mood for the rest of the game.

Now, most of us probably would choose drinks over our own flesh and blood, but the reality is that life does happen sometimes, and situations can lead us to make rash, poorly judged decisions that may not always affect us directly, but those around us. It's okay to not be okay sometimes, but the ultimate consequence should always be in view.

THEY CAN AFFECT YOUR HEALTH AND WELL-BEING

Certain decisions can directly affect your health and general well-being. Some of these decisions are ones you make automatically because you are accustomed to them, and have incorporated them into a soothing habit like finishing an entire bottle of wine when you are under pressure. It easily becomes your coping mechanism and might work for the moment, but in the long run, it can lead to severe health issues. Having a glass or two isn't detrimental, but when you have decided to use it as your only way to get things done is where it gets muddy.

Drinking doesn't have to be the only decision that has consequences on your mental and physical health, too. But if your mind and body are screaming at you silently, then you might want to wake up and reanalyze your decision-making.

THEY CAN AFFECT PRODUCTIVITY

It is no secret that poor decisions can affect your productivity negatively, and this, more than any other consequence, could worsen our overthinking even more. Not being able to feel productive due to being in a rut about a bad decision, or picking up the pieces of a bad decision, we might fall back on work or school, leaving us even more stressed than before. This, of course, can make your overthinking worse, or at the very least, stop it from going away.

AFFECT YOUR SELF-ESTEEM AND CONFIDENCE

We have all probably been there, when we feel on top of the world when the decision we've made turned out to be a great one. However, in the same way, making poor decisions can turn your self-esteem and confidence into mush. This is because your self-perception is strongly influenced by a variety of decisions. Even deciding to engage in negative self-talk is a choice (which is a habit of most overthinkers), and doing so lowers your self-esteem, which makes it simpler to keep making the same decision.

But when you are conscious of your thoughts, you can make wiser decisions. Consider the repercussions of dwelling on the negative versus focusing on the positive.

For example, you can decide to read self-uplifting affirmations carefully and realize that it's okay to enjoy things in moderation instead of blaming yourself mentally for eating that cookie.

THEY CAN AFFECT YOUR LEGAL SITUATION AND PERMANENT RECORD

Making poor decisions may affect your legal situation or even your permanent record. Even a little offense can have long-term repercussions for you and those involved. More serious offenses may result in incarceration, the loss of your ability to vote, as well as severe financial strain for you and your family.

For example, deciding to steal a candy bar from a store rather than paying for it may seem like a small decision, but can yield serious consequences.

BETTER DECISION-MAKING

We all occasionally have to make important decisions. It can be challenging to decide which road to choose when thinking about changing careers, deciding whether to begin a family or struggling with any other major decision.

If you had a magic ball to guide you in those choices, things would be much simpler. Unfortunately, that's not how life works. It is a little bit more difficult to know for sure that you are making the right choice in reality. It calls for a great deal of good judgment and even some risk-taking, both of which can be frightening and overwhelming.

It can, however, also be thrilling. The possibilities are unlimited since you have the freedom to make your own decisions. If you give yourself permission, you can be who you want to be and do whatever you desire instead of being trapped in the mental prison that overthinking has kept you.

Even while you can't just wave a magic wand and have those difficult decisions made for you, you may use these steps and strategies to get started.

3 STEPS TO MAKING GOOD DECISIONS

You can make more careful, intelligent decisions by gathering information and outlining alternatives. This strategy raises the likelihood that you'll select the one that will satisfy you the most, reduce the consequences and help avoid and/or control overthinking.

STEP 1: COLLECT THE RELEVANT INFORMATION

It is imperative that you gather all of the relevant facts and information before making any choice.

For instance, in order for you to choose a seat on the aircraft you're taking for your next business trip, it was necessary to know whether or not the trip was completely booked. With this piece of information, you would be able to decide whether or not to choose a seat in the middle of the aisle, where there is a possibility that you'll be stuck in the middle.

The number of individuals who would ultimately board the plane was an important consideration in making the optimal decision. So, you would inquire with the flight attendant, and she would probably tell you that the plane would be rather crowded.

Ultimately, the key to success in this situation is to first collect the information and then go to the next stage.

STEP 2: MAKE SENSE OF THE FACTS

Now that you have all of the necessary information, it is time to interpret it so you can come to a conclusion and make a decision. In the instance of the airplane seat, the interpretation was clear: You couldn't rely on having an empty seat next to you, therefore, you would choose your seat in accordance with that reality.

When it comes to making decisions for our businesses or lives, one of the pitfalls we might fall prey to is allowing uncertainty and fear to influence our judgment. Don't let those feelings get to you. You should base your decision on the facts as you currently understand them.

STEP 3: EVALUATE THE OPPORTUNITIES AND OPTIONS, AND MAKE A SELECTION

You've investigated your alternatives; now it's time to use your creativity and examine the various possibilities available to you. The time for choosing a path forward has arrived. If you've completed steps 1 and 2, you should be able to determine which option is best. Create it, and then get started putting it into action. Try not to second-guess your own judgment.

You might want to go through the procedure again to reach a different option if the choice did not satisfy the indicated need. For instance, you could want to obtain information that is more specific or significantly different or consider more options.

THREE WAYS OVERTHINKERS CAN MAKE GOOD DECISIONS

Overthinking typically manifests as a distressed expression and an endless mental conversation about your choices. Here are a few go-to methods for reducing overthinking so you can make better judgments.

ASK FOR ADVICE

Sometimes, as humans we might be reluctant to ask for advice, help, or tips on something. But, indeed, we are not going to know everything ourselves, and especially when you notice that you have a habit of overthinking, asking for advice on a decision gives you assurance and confidence to make this choice, without spending countless hours overthinking afterward. But be certain to ask people who are knowledgeable in the area that you want to make the decision on, so that it can be as sound as possible.

ESTABLISH BENEFICIAL CONSTRAINTS

Have you ever given yourself a month to complete a project, and it actually took you the entire month? Later, you were given only seven days to do the identical assignment, yet you still managed to complete it in that short amount of time. Crazy, right?

This occurs as a result of overthinking growing as long as we let it. This is precisely why setting rules and accountability can help you make good decisions quickly and without hesitation.

According to the Association of Talent Development, simply committing to something or telling someone else about it enhances your chances of success by up to 95% (Wayne, 2021).

Setting external limitations trains your brain to behave more quickly and spend less time thinking. Setting time limits on how long you spend on each task is one approach to this. For instance, setting a timer for 25 minutes, working until the bell rings, and then taking a 5-minute break are the steps involved in this. You've earned a 15-minute break after four sessions.

It also helps to set a deadline for yourself. Choose a period or date by which you will make the decision. Schedule a reminder on your phone, add it to your calendar, or even better, get in touch with the person who is waiting for your choice and let them know when to anticipate a response from you.

One of the easiest methods to make sure you follow through is to publicly commit to a deadline in a meeting or via email.

If you find yourself mired in contemplation, you can get the help of others by setting up a talk with a coworker, your manager, a mentor, or a friend. This will encourage you to arrange and summarize the data that you have gathered in the process, and tackle the thoughts that have been circling in your mind in a clear, succinct manner.

FOLLOW YOUR GUT

Yes, it's true that sometimes our "gut" isn't the best thing to make a sound decision. But a feeling, an urge, or a deeper understanding regarding a decision can help. The term "gut feelings" is the capacity to comprehend things intuitively without using conscious thought.

In other words, you receive solutions and answers even though you might not fully understand their origin or purpose.

Trusting your instincts often receives a bad rap in the era of big data. It's common to dismiss intuition—the term used to describe gut instincts in research—as mystical or unreliable. While it's true that intuition can often be mistaken for something else, studies have shown that using both logical thinking and your gut sensations together can increase your decision-making efficiency and confidence (Wayne, 2021). This is especially true when there are multiple "right" options or when you are overthinking the situation.

In fact, surveys of senior executives reveal that the vast majority of leaders use their intuition and past experiences to manage crises. Exactly because intuition can outweigh intelligence in high-stakes scenarios like the battlefield, the U.S. Navy has spent millions of dollars assisting sailors and Marines in honing their sixth sense (Wayne, 2021).

The good news is that intuition is like a muscle, even though you may have been taught to disregard your gut instincts. With deliberate repetition, it can be strengthened.

Making simple choices is a terrific place to begin. Without considering too many factors, pick an outfit that speaks to you. In a meeting, raise your hand and speak up without holding back. You become accustomed to using your intuition by acting swiftly and decisively with few consequences.

By beginning small, you can reduce feelings of overwhelm and build up your confidence as you gradually move up to bigger, more stressful decisions. This strategy works because it increases your capacity for emotional self-regulation under stressful circumstances, and lessens the impact of overthinking.

HOW TO DETERMINE WHETHER YOUR DECISION IS THE RIGHT ONE

Only you have the true ability to determine what is best for you. If you feel genuinely happy after making a decision, and your concise, "gut" or heart is hurting after you've made a choice, you are on the right road to knowing that it was the right one for you.

Many times, we are faced with a situation of making a decision that others around us might be upset about. But if it was the right choice for you, there should be no reason for you to feel as though you've done a bad thing.

These additional indicators can assist you in figuring out whether the direction you're taking aligns with your true goals.

YOUR INSTINCTS SAY IT'S RIGHT

Again, there is merit in following your instincts. That inner voice will frequently tell you to do what seems right.

That small voice might be quieter than usual as a result of things like overthinking, evaluating yourself in comparison to others, and outside stimuli. But it's worth believing your inner voice if it's telling you that you're making the right choice.

The same is true when you have a sneaking suspicion that you're making the wrong decision. Perhaps you experience pressure to make a decision that just doesn't feel right for you. That is also entirely valid.

CONSIDERING YOUR VALUES

It can be challenging to follow your gut instincts when the voice in your head is barely audible. Making it louder can be achieved by taking some time to consider what is genuinely important to you.

Reflection techniques that work well include prayer, meditation, journaling, creating art, and spending time in nature. Use whatever makes sense to you, even if it isn't on this list.

Consider your values after you've given yourself this peaceful time. Think about how your choice either upholds or violates your values, whatever they may be.

IMAGINE TWO POTENTIAL OUTCOMES

Once self-doubt has taken hold, it can be challenging to escape its vicious cycle. Even while it's normal to think about potential consequences before making a choice, you might not be aware that your mind tends to concentrate more on the bad than the good.

If this applies to you, set a goal for yourself to consider some optimistic "what ifs." For instance, if you frequently wonder, *What if I don't like the new city I'm going to?* kindly allow yourself to consider the scenario, *What if I adore it? What if I meet a ton of new people? What if I enjoy discovering new areas around me?*

LOOKING OVER YOUR LIFE

When faced with a difficult decision, it might feel all-consuming. Though it's necessary to give decisions, especially significant ones, serious consideration, you also face the risk of overthinking. Too much time spent thinking about your circumstance could prevent you from acting.

Gently take a step back and widen the scope of your life if you feel like you are drowning in worried thoughts about your choice. Assure yourself that this is only one of many decisions you will face (and have already faced!) throughout your lifetime.

This choice won't make or break your life, despite how it might feel right now. You will create it into what you want.

THINK ABOUT WHAT YOU'D TELL YOUR FRIEND

Everything always feels different when it's happening to us specifically. Consider the counsel you'd give a friend in this situation if the roles had been reversed.

How would you help a friend make this decision if they were in the same situation? Do you believe they are acting in their own best interests?

Although this method isn't error-free, it might assist you in viewing your issue more objectively. Theoretically, you wouldn't have to agree with every decision your friend makes, but using this technique can help you gain a new viewpoint on whether your decision is sound.

9

OVERCOME OVERTHINKING BY BUILDING SELF-ESTEEM

Self-esteem is crucial in the modern world when information, skills, and creativity are the most valuable assets on the market. Innovation, inventiveness, and self-assurance in our abilities will be absent and growth will be limited without self-esteem. It is, therefore, one of the most valuable aspects of self that we can have, next to self-love and self-compassion.

Our degree of self-esteem is reflected in how we behave at work, how we interact with others, how we handle problems, and the partners we pick. A healthy sense of self-pride, a certain tone of voice, the ability to assert ourselves, and the ability to balance our demands with those of others are all signs of high self-esteem.

Self-esteem is not the same as arrogance or narcissism, as some people may believe. People with strong self-esteem have high standards, are entirely independent, respect other people, and actively seek out methods to uplift them. Like there is no such thing as too much good health, there is no such thing as having too much self-esteem.

So, how does this relate to overthinking? Having low self-esteem makes us feel as if we're a victim. We might feel like our hands are tied behind our backs, and this causes us to start to *think* that we can't do what we want or intended to do. This constant pattern of thinking might lead to ruminating and excessive thought, known as overthinking.

Self-esteem affects the happiness level that you achieve in your life. Therefore, in this chapter, we will examine and briefly discuss six facets of developing self-esteem.

THE PRACTICE OF LIVING CONSCIOUSLY

A fundamental pillar of self-esteem is the practice of living consciously. What is this, exactly? Living consciously means taking responsibility for your life, giving careful consideration to your choices rather than acting on impulse, and working toward the kind of life you envision for yourself rather than accepting the life that is thrust upon you.

We can increase our chances of being happy, healthier, and more successful in life by adopting a lifestyle that emphasizes conscious living. However, it is not something that can be accomplished overnight; the journey to achieve consciousness and contentment is one that requires time as well as a lot of concentrated effort, which in the end, can be the first step in building self-esteem.

We need to become more conscious of our daily behaviors. Are we just going through the motions, sleeping through life, and neglecting all the places where we know we might be doing better? When we are aware that we are not comfortable at our jobs but lack the bravery to change careers, we sometimes feel anxious. Or when we enjoy our work but are aware that we are not giving our best effort.

Our consciousness level can also be seen in the quality of our interactions with others. Are we truly there, or are we only physically present but spiritually entirely absent?

Sentence-completion exercises are an incredibly successful method for improving self-awareness, self-worth, and personal efficacy. It is based on the idea that everyone has more knowledge than they often realize, more wisdom than they employ, and more potential than they typically demonstrate in their actions. A tool for gaining access to and using these "hidden resources" is sentence completion.

Here's the basic idea: Create six to ten sentence-completion stems, such as "Living mindfully to me means..." The only requirement is that every conclusion must result in a grammatical statement. Any ending is acceptable, so just keep writing. Write quickly and don't pause to consider.

Try these on for size:

- If I increase my awareness of my actions today...

- If I'm more mindful of how I interact with people now...

- If I increase the awareness of my insecurities, then...

- If I increase my awareness of my priorities, then...

Our level of happiness and sense of self will change as our consciousness grows each day as a result of our commitment to bringing more awareness to our daily actions.

THE PRACTICE OF SELF-ACCEPTANCE

The need for self-acceptance implies that we can run not just from our dark side but from our positive side—from everything that threatens to make us stick out or stand-alone, or that urges the hero inside us to awaken, or requires that we break through to a greater level of awareness and achieve a higher ground of integrity. The biggest wrong we do to ourselves is to reject and disavow our brilliance because it terrifies us, not because we may deny or disown our flaws.

In addition to accepting our light, being conscious of and accepting disowned portions of the self does as much for your self-esteem as

146

anything else. Acceptance and awareness—also known as mindfulness and integration—are the initial steps in healing and progress.

Accepting every aspect of your personality, your circumstances, your weaknesses, and even the physical qualities you despise most about yourself is part of the process of self-acceptance (yes, even the crooked nose and the baby fat). This is the simplest thing to accomplish, yet it could very well be the most difficult. If you have ever been the victim of bullying, you probably don't feel comfortable in your own skin. Signs include nervousness, a sense of unworthiness, and a lack of assertiveness (even in the workplace).

Self-acceptance does not mean complacency; rather, it is accepting the bad things, such as the fact that you are not giving your all, that you could lack managerial skills, that you lack organization, or that you are experiencing feelings of inadequacy. When you have mastered this, you will be able to address your weaknesses, which will be extremely beneficial to your sense of self-worth.

Accept the excellent aspects in yourself, such as your marketing talents, your capacity to comfort those around you with a simple joke or smile, and your sharpness in finding solutions to problems. In the same regard, accept the good things about yourself. Increasing your proficiency in this area will make you feel better about yourself.

THE PRACTICE OF SELF-RESPONSIBILITY

To be "responsible" in this context implies being accountable for the major and minor factors in your life and actions, not "responsible" as the object of moral blame or guilt.

Think of a situation where you came up with an idea that could send your company on the charts! Your manager loves it, your team loves it, and you take full responsibility for that idea. But if the situation was reversed, would you do the same?

We can only be said to be responsible when we can respond to the difficulties of life as strong, independent persons, rather than as victims who place blame on others or external factors. We must, therefore, feel in charge of our life if we are to feel capable of living and deserving of happiness.

The moment we begin blaming the world, the state, our parents, or even God, we lose willpower, self-control, power, and most of all, self-esteem. You are in charge of your happiness, the fulfillment of your goals, your decisions and their results, the standard of your work, and the nature of your relationships.

It can be challenging to think for ourselves at times because of our upbringing, but we must mature. Be accountable for what you can manage to achieve your beliefs, goals, and aspirations. Don't limit yourself to low self-esteem, by refusing to accept accountability.

THE PRACTICE OF ASSERTIVENESS

Self-assertiveness is living truthfully, speaking and acting from your innermost thoughts and feelings. Being authentic is the cornerstone of this pillar. Being true to yourself means writing your own story, and being the author of the history that everyone around you will know. Do you see this to be a good story?

Self-assertiveness involves assertively putting yourself out there and communicating your opinions and ideals in the appropriate situations. People with low self-esteem frequently refrain from expressing their opinions or don't stand up for them when they are opposed. For example, practicing good assertiveness in the workplace would be standing firm on your idea of adapting a hybridized platform, even when the senior managers oppose it.

Perhaps they, like you, have their reasons, but this level of assertiveness demonstrates high self-esteem in its true form. You would be surprised that it is this very level of self-esteem that makes them push your idea forward, and even gives you a promotion.

People with poor self-esteem often convey facts or ideas in a way that makes their tone sound questionable at the conclusion of the sentence, or they suppress themselves out of concern of taking up too much space. That is one way that a lack of self-esteem might show up. Unfortunately, certain cultures encourage this kind of self-suppression, and anyone expressing self-esteem or assertiveness is branded as conceited or selfish.

However, the secret to this technique is to assert yourself with confidence while still showing respect for others. We must push ourselves to communicate our thoughts, question established norms, and face rejection without fear.

THE PRACTICE OF LIVING PURPOSEFULLY

To live meaningfully is to use our abilities to fulfill goals we have selected such as the purpose of learning, raising a family, starting a new business, solving a family mystery, buying a vacation home, or sustaining a successful romantic relationship. Our goals are what drive us ahead, require the use of our abilities, and give our life meaning.

So what are your goals? What truly motivates you? The visions that strongly resonate with your greatest values and aspirations are not the things that you think will impress other people; it is only what matters to your purpose.

People hardly ever ask themselves, "If my goal is to have a happy family, what must I do? What steps must be taken to establish and maintain intimacy, ongoing self-disclosure, excitement, and growth?"

Instead, we usually just dive right in. But take a minute and think about what is really meaningful to you, and what must be done to achieve this. What do you want, to begin with? What is necessary for you to do? Purposes unrelated to an action plan do not materialize. They exist as unfulfilled dreams.

Therefore, to live intentionally means to transform our dreams and goals into particular activities that advance the achievement of those goals.

Purpose can also be found in daily activities such as parenting, spending time with loved ones, and developing a passion. Being productive and effective is easier the more obvious our purpose is.

The key to this practice is learning self-discipline—the capacity to put off comfort and immediate enjoyment in favor of a brighter future. This doesn't imply that there isn't time for relaxation, but rather that people choose to pursue their purpose voluntarily.

PERSONAL INTEGRITY

Integrity is the combination of thoughts, convictions, standards, beliefs, and actions that upholds what is right. The consistency of our actions with our values, ideals, and convictions is referred to as personal integrity. We are honest when they line up. When we act in a way that goes against our judgment, even if no one else notices, we regard ourselves less, hindering our self-esteem.

For instance, being nice to someone when others are watching, but being mean behind closed doors is poor integrity. Our integrity is demonstrated when our actions are consistent with the beliefs we claim to uphold. Even if no one else is aware, lying, cheating, and mistreating others can be damaging to your self-esteem. Mistreating employees while constantly extolling the virtues of integrity is another example.

Do your values, beliefs, standards, and actions align with your ideals? Better question: Do you even know what your values, convictions, standards, and beliefs are? This is maybe even more crucial.

Do you walk the walk? When you speak, do you mean what you say? Take a minute to consider how your words and actions match up—or don't—with the definition of integrity.

10

OVERCOME OVERTHINKING BY DITCHING NEGATIVE THOUGHTS

N egative thinking can be a factor in issues including low self-esteem, sadness, stress, and social anxiety. Understanding how you think currently (and the issues that occur) is the key to changing your negative thoughts. After that, utilize techniques to alter these thoughts or lessen their impact.

Our thoughts affect how we feel and act since they are connected to our emotions and behaviors. Therefore, even if we all occasionally have negative thoughts, it's crucial to know what to do in order to prevent them from dictating how our day will go.

In this final chapter, we will leave with a bang by discussing the facets of negative thoughts, which are completely different from the negative emotions that we covered in Chapter 4. We will also observe how to tackle these negative thoughts that usually encourage or maintain overthinking, and move into a positive, bright future.

IDENTIFYING NEGATIVE THOUGHTS

Unconscious negative thought frequently serves as the foundation for some of our undesirable behavior. But how can you become conscious of the thoughts you are having but aren't even aware of?

Understanding your negative thought patterns can give you the skills you need to stop intrusive thoughts and develop a more positive outlook on life. Negative thoughts can be changed, but first, you must learn to identify the patterns of bad thinking that underlie your negative sensations and behaviors.

CHARACTERISTICS OF NEGATIVE THINKING

You may not know it yet, but being able to identify what a negative thought looks like is the first step to overcoming it in the first place. Take, for example, the types of overthinking. When you learned them, did it not help you identify which one is most prevalent in your life, and help give you an upper hand in beating it? The same is true here. So, here are five characteristics of negative thinking to get you started:

- **Automatic:** These negative thoughts are without any conscious effort on your part; they merely appear in your thoughts. For example, you might be sitting in traffic and without you knowing it, you start thinking about all the possibilities of an accident happening. You didn't conjure this thought, but it appeared from the situation that you were currently in. These thoughts can be harmful, especially if you give them the time or space to manifest into more than just a "what if," but an entire fear.

- **Derailed:** These negative thoughts don't match all the evidence or are simply incorrect in general. We all might have experienced this before. For instance, thinking that a UFO will appear out of nowhere and aliens will invade the planet. Perhaps you are so prone to always thinking about the negative and overthinking in general, that you find all manner of negativity to consider.

- **Helpless:** These thoughts have an impact on your emotions and actions. They make it challenging for you to change and prevent you from achieving your goals in life. This is similar to the type of overthinking—hopelessness—which gives you a sense of despair when considering action.

- **Accurate:** These negative thoughts might be the most harmful. They occur when you believe them to be true and do not think to challenge them. For instance, you might believe that you can never learn to ride a bike because you had fallen so many times when you were a child. Now, you are dead set on the notion that you can never learn.

- **Intrusive:** These negative thoughts are not your choice, they might be upsetting or aggressive, and they can be very difficult to turn off. They can come about by being around negative people, being in a situation where all you can do is worry (like hearing that your loved one met with a car accident), or experiencing something heartbreaking.

12 SIGNS FOR IDENTIFYING NEGATIVE THOUGHTS

How do you know if you are having negative thoughts? Who knows, perhaps you believe that a thought is simply "motivating," when in truth, it is a negative thought giving out a false drive to go forward.

Therefore, in this section, we will look at different techniques to identify negative thoughts when they arise.

SEEING IN BLACK AND WHITE

You can identify negative thinking by assessing if you are missing the gray and seeing everything in black and white. For example, *My new coworkers either adore me or detest me.*

PUTTING SITUATIONS IN THE SAME BOX

If you are interpreting one bad experience as an indication that everything is bad, then you are possibly having a negative thought. For example, saying *I always fail, because I fail at everything I do* or *I will always and forever be in debt because life is hard.*

MENTAL SCREENING

When you find yourself choosing a single negative aspect and concentrating solely on it, disregarding any potential positives, this is a negative thought. For instance, after a chat, you only remember one minor critique and disregard the 16 positive things that person said.

LEAVING OUT THE POSITIVE

Noticing a positive aspect of your life but dismissing it as unimportant is another sign of negative thinking. You may think it's not relevant or "anyone can do that."

MAKING HASTY JUDGMENTS

When you find yourself making judgments without supporting evidence, that is negative is another indicator. For example, you might say, *My gland is swollen; it must be cancer*.

ASSUMING WHAT OTHERS THINK

You might have negative thoughts when you start interpreting other people's possible thoughts negatively. *Everyone thought I was stupid in that presentation there, I'm to blame*. While accepting responsibility for your part is necessary, placing too much blame on yourself is counterproductive. Watch out for moments when you persuade yourself that something is "all your fault" or that you "ruined everything."

TRYING TO FIND BAD NEWS

It's easy to concentrate on the only negative event in a day when nine positives and one negative occur. However, focusing on the bad will just keep you there.

SPECULATING

You might "predict" doom and gloom even if you have no idea what will occur tomorrow. Negative speculation can, if you're not careful, become a self-fulfilling prophecy, whether you imagine that you'll embarrass yourself in a presentation or tell yourself that you will never get a promotion.

MAGNIFYING

You might find yourself exaggerating the significance of situations like errors in a negative way. For example, maybe you accidentally reverse into the curb in the parking lot, and on your way home that same evening, you keep thinking that the entire car bumper will fall off. As unlikely as it is, since it was a small hit, your mind blows it up even more than it initially was.

MINIMIZATION

When you underestimate the significance of happy occasions or your own excellent traits, you might tend to think negatively. For example, it might be the first day at your new job, you meet a coworker and you instantly hit it off. However, your thoughts might be, *She seems to like my company, but that is only because I am new here.* This, in and of itself, is negative thinking.

SELF-BLAME

You hold yourself accountable for certain unfounded externally-caused negative events. Remember that you are accountable for your own thoughts and feelings while others are accountable for their own. But, you might be thinking negatively when you say something like, "I'm just bad luck for anyone who gets near me."

PUTTING YOURSELF DOWN

Putting a bad reputation on yourself with your thoughts basically screams negative thinking. *I'm lousy, I don't deserve any better, or I am foolish, untrustworthy, and weak*, are just a few of these thoughts.

You may experience negative thoughts if you can relate to at least three of these negative thought patterns. Remember that much of this thinking happens unconsciously, so it can be challenging to identify it. Given that everyone has a mind, it's likely that we all occasionally have negative thoughts. However, if they are bothersome or intrusive, it may be time to question these mental patterns.

TYPES OF NEGATIVE THOUGHTS

Try to identify any of these harmful thought patterns within your own thinking, and if you do, note how frequently you do it. Try to pay close attention to your thoughts throughout the coming days and weeks to see if you can spot any of the following.

Even if the list may seem lengthy, it is advisable to go through it all so that we can recognize when we are thinking these types of thoughts.

EMOTIONAL JUDGMENT

This kind of destructive thinking occurs when we believe that something is true despite the fact that the only evidence we have to support this belief is the feeling that it elicits in us. It might be difficult to have a productive discourse with someone who is emotionally reasoning since they tend to concentrate more on their unfavorable sentiments than they do on logical considerations. The emotional reasoner starts with the presumption that there must be a problem since they are experiencing negative feelings, and then they fabricate a story to demonstrate that the problem does in fact exist.

Consider the case of a man who is convinced, despite the absence of any evidence to the contrary, that his coworkers detest him. Then, he builds on this narrative by reading too much into any encounters or conversations he has with them, only noticing the times when he feels they are being unfriendly and ignoring the times when he feels they are being good to him. This leads him to believe that they do not like him and that they are trying to get him into trouble.

BEING EXAGGERATIVE

This type of negative thinking focuses on a single troubling aspect or experience and gives it undue weight. By doing this, we frequently discount partial successes or accomplishments.

For instance, Gary attends a job interview but receives no response later. Then, instead of realizing that there will be other possibilities in the future and that the employer must have found something admirable in him to invite him to an interview, he begins to believe he will never work again.

LABELING

This includes viewing our surroundings, the other people in our lives, or even ourselves in a negative light. It is common practice to apply labels such as "loser," "idiot," "terrible person," "terrible parent," "typical man or woman," and so on. By applying these labels, we impose restrictions on ourselves and stop ourselves from growing.

Let's say for the sake of argument that a friend turns down an invitation from a guy to hang out over the weekend on the grounds that their schedule is already jam-packed. On the other hand, he convinces himself, "I must be a loser" because he did not start making preparations earlier.

Or, to give yet another illustration, consider the scenario in which a father is late to pick up his child from school and finds that the vast majority of the other children have already been collected. He considers himself to be a "lousy father," even though there was a valid explanation for why he was late.

ADVANCE CONCLUSIONS

This is forming an opinion or "snap judgment" about something quickly and negatively without considering all the facts or gathering sufficient data.

For example, Louis texts a friend to ask whether he's available that night, but he doesn't immediately get a response. Louis, therefore, assumes that his friend is deliberately ignoring him and no longer wants to be friends.

CONSCIOUS FILTERING

This is choosing (consciously or unconsciously) to keep in mind only the negative aspects of an event.

An athlete who is depressed can, for instance, forget his many outstanding plays and focus instead on the one error he made.

FORECASTING AND FORTUNE TELLING

This means repeatedly forecasting that situations won't go well. When we project our negativity onto the future, it can become a self-fulfilling prophecy where our inability to act in a way that would produce positive results happens.

For instance, a lady may be feeling lonely and may not have as many close friends as she would like. Then, she envisioned this emotion into the future and concluded that she will never gain new connections. She then feels even more alone and prevents herself from trying to form new friendships by believing this to be true.

MIND READING

This idea, which can also be understood as an example of overthinking, was initially presented to us in chapter one. When we believe this, we are assuming that we have a perfect understanding of what the thoughts and feelings of another person are, particularly regarding you.

For instance, believing that someone dislikes you because they gave you a hostile response to a question you posed, rather than considering the possibility that they were flustered or concerned with something unrelated to the situation in which they found themselves.

NEVER WRONG

Everyone wants to be right, but this desire is distorted when it takes precedence over facts, logic, and reality.

As an illustration, a father enters the incorrect time for his son's dental appointment. When his spouse confronts him about the missing appointment, he refuses to own up to it and says that either she failed to inform him at the appropriate time or that the dentist's office made a mistake on their end.

CONTROL FALLACIES

There are two ways a control fallacy could appear:

- Feeling hopeless because you believe you have no control over anything in your life and are unable to make any changes.

- Feeling hopeless because you believe you should have complete control over every aspect of your life and are, hence, solely at fault for any unfortunate or challenging situation.

For instance, having the impression that you have no control over your profession and are unable to change your situation. Or, believing that you are solely to blame for your dismissal and that you should have worked more despite the fact that the company filed for bankruptcy and everyone lost their jobs regardless of job performance.

FAIRNESS IGNORANCE

The saying, "The world isn't fair" is typically used in response to someone who is having difficulty with the fallacy of fairness. In the context of our mental health, it is frequently not useful to evaluate circumstances in terms of how fair or unfair they might be.

Take, for instance, a situation where despite putting in extra time and doing well, office politics prevent a man from getting promoted at work. Then he starts to think negatively and keeps thinking about how unfair it feels. Even though the situation may not be fair, dwelling on the "fairness" of our condition keeps us from going forward.

HIDING THE GOOD

This means asserting that happy experiences "don't count" in order to reject or discount them. Life is less enjoyable when the positive is discounted.

For instance, if a friend compliments your clothing, you could not feel good about it since you assume they are merely saying it out of obligation and don't really appreciate it.

BLAMING SELF

Making ourselves, our feelings, or our involvement in events out of facts that have nothing to do with us.

For example, when a child unjustly holds themselves responsible for their parents' divorce or when we place all the responsibility for something's failure on ourselves while dismissing other possible causes.

"MUST" OR "SHOULD"

This is self-criticism and self-judging based on what we believe we "should" or "must" have done.

For instance, a person who experiences anxiety when speaking on the phone could criticize themselves because they feel they "should" be able to have a simple phone call without getting tense. They become more frustrated with themselves, believing that this shouldn't be a problem for them, rather than striving to control their anxiousness when speaking on the phone.

RUMINATING OR OVERTHINKING

Alas, we have stumbled upon our most common frenemy in this book.

We are stewing or ruminating when we find ourselves continuously running over things in our minds, almost as if we were in a loop, without any new knowledge being obtained or action being performed. In most cases, this only results in the problems at hand expanding in scope and becoming more difficult to manage.

Especially when dealing with thoughts of sadness, which typically involve a combination of many of the thought patterns stated above, this is a highly common and damaging habit to adopt, and it is especially problematic when dealing with thoughts of sadness.

For instance, a man may experience feelings of humiliation as a direct result of a mistake he has made or a hasty comment that he has made. When he thinks about all of the times that he has screwed up or done something embarrassing, it makes him feel even more unhappy than he already was. Eventually, he starts to forget about all of the good things that life has to offer.

It is crucial to the management of negative thoughts to recognize when they first appear. As soon as we become conscious of our negative ideas, we may start to eliminate, lessen, or somehow reframe them.

CONSEQUENCES OF NEGATIVE THINKING

Life is not always easy. But when we think negatively, we make things harder. We're referring to the tendency to always see the glass as half-empty and to focus primarily on its shortcomings rather than its virtues. So, let's get started with that in mind.

Negative thoughts have a wide-ranging impact. It affects every aspect of your life. You experience mental, emotional, and physical effects from it, and restricts your capacity for success and enjoyment of life.

Here are just a few of such consequences.

AFFECTS YOUR ATTITUDE ON LIFE

Negative thinking can cause negative emotions like sadness, fear, anger, hopelessness, and negativity all in one. Your perspective of the world can then be tainted by these feelings. When everyone and everything is "out to get you," you will, at best, be cautious and untrusting. Because you are anticipating a bad thing to happen, you could be reluctant to try anything new or to speak up. You might also decide not to take advantage of possibilities because of negative thinking.

AFFECTS GOAL-SETTING

There are forces pushing you in one direction and others dragging you away from any purpose. When you have negative thoughts about achieving a goal, your chances of success are significantly reduced.

Imagine that you'd like to travel to a faraway exotic location that is still very far from where you are right now (if you feel secure doing so). But then you start to think, *The jet lag will be terrible; it's so far away. The language is really dissimilar. How will I get by? I ought to use the funds for something else; The exchange rate will cost me a lot of money.*

That ideal journey to that far-off place now doesn't sound so fantastic. Goals appear more difficult than they actually are when you think negatively.

IT UNDERMINES YOUR CONFIDENCE

Your self-confidence suffers when you think negatively about yourself. For instance, your self-esteem and confidence are damaged when you believe that you are overweight, unfit, ugly, unable, or that you have given yourself any other negative term.

DEPRESSION-RELATED EMOTIONS

Negative thinking might exacerbate depressive symptoms. This might be quite harmful if left unchecked. For example, constantly thinking that you are a loser can feed into already present negative emotions, and become something worse, like depression.

CAUSES RELATIONSHIP DIFFICULTIES

A failure to communicate and even a "playful" level of criticism can have harmful effects, whether the continual self-criticism makes you come out as needy and insecure or you transfer your negative thinking further into general negative behaviors that annoy others. This, therefore, can affect how you interact with others around you, and may even cause others to pull away from your "negative energy."

STRATEGIES FOR COMBATING NEGATIVE THOUGHTS

You can cut back on your negative thinking in a variety of ways. Recognize your own self-criticism so you can learn to quit it. Although having negative thoughts about yourself may seem like wise insights, they are most definitely not reliable sources of information.

Try out a few different ones to find which one works best for you. Different tactics are more effective for different people, so what works for a friend might not work for you. Feel free to experiment with these six strategies for fighting negative thoughts.

INTERROGATE YOUR INNER CRITIC

The fact that negative thinking frequently goes unchecked is one of its destructive qualities. Since it's happening inside your head, it's possible that nobody can correct you if you're wrong because they aren't aware of what you're saying.

Catching your negative thoughts and evaluating their accuracy is significantly preferable. The bulk of negative thoughts are an exaggeration; therefore, recognizing this might help lessen their harmful effects.

You can also give your inner critic a nickname. For instance, when you have a negative thought, say, *Oh hey, Josy. That's not true and I won't believe it.*

CONSIDER YOUR FRIENDS

At its worst, our inner critic can resemble our fiercest enemy. Think about the instances in which you have a conversation with yourself in a manner that you would never use with a child or a close friend. It is hurtful to the ear, isn't it? Similarly, you are causing harm to yourself. Why not flip this around and make it a point to visualize saying this to a great friend whenever you catch yourself thinking negatively? If you do this, you will find that your outlook on life will improve.

Consider how a good friend may respond to you or how you would like to be addressed by a good friend if you are positive that you would not express yourself in this manner. If you are convinced that you would not, then consider how a good friend might respond to you. Changing the way you typically think can be accomplished quite well by using this method.

CHANGE YOUR VIEWPOINT

It's possible that unless you take a more holistic picture of the circumstances, you aren't giving anything the attention it deserves. Consider whether the issue at hand will still be relevant in five years or even one year from now if you find yourself indignant about something.

As yet another strategy for altering your point of view, you might give some thought to zooming out and examining the problems you're facing from a very far away. If you see the world as a globe and yourself as an incredibly little speck on that globe, you will be reminded that the majority of the challenges you face are not nearly as severe as they might initially appear. This often helps to minimize the hurriedness, dread, and pessimism that are associated with negative thinking.

Take a moment to think back on a time in your life when you did something that made you look foolish. You wince in discomfort no matter where you think about it. Now, think about if anyone else recalls besides you. In certain instances, there may be one or two people who have exceptional memory, but in the vast majority of cases, the issue has moved on, and it will no longer have any bearing on you.

SPEAKING ALOUD

When you catch yourself having negative thoughts, it can be helpful to simply say them out loud. When we share something personal with a close friend we can count on to be trustworthy, it often leads to a good laugh that sheds light on how ridiculous some of our negative thoughts can be. At the very least, it offers support in certain situations.

Even the act of silently muttering such self-defeating phrases can serve as a helpful reminder of how absurd they appear. This will serve as a prompt to take some time off and relax for yourself.

PUT THAT THOUGHT TO REST

Simply putting an end to negative thoughts can be beneficial for some people. When a bad idea enters your head, you can "think-stop" it by snapping a rubber band on your wrist (not to hurt yourself), picturing a stop sign, literally saying "stop" aloud, or just switching to another one. This can be beneficial when dealing with negative or recurrent thoughts, such as, *I'm no good* or *I'll never be able to do this*, for instance.

PUT SOME GOOD IN PLACE OF THE BAD

One of the most effective ways to deal with negative thoughts is replacing them with a superior alternative. Transform a pessimistic thought into an inspiring and true statement. For example, when you think, *I'm a failure*, replace it by saying, *I'm improving*. Even if the positive alternative isn't 100% true as yet, still say it until it is.

Repeat until you find that you need to do it progressively less frequently. Most negative habits can be broken by doing this; for instance, substituting good foods for unhealthy ones. It's a terrific way to cultivate a more optimistic outlook on life and yourself.

Your life can be significantly improved proactively by reducing the inclination you have to think negatively. Negative thinking can cause you to lose happiness in life, as well as success and even your health. Invest some time in making sure that the thoughts running through your head are positive and encouraging for yourself and others so that you can start to see the potential in everything.

CONCLUSION

It is not exactly a well-kept secret that excessive thinking may be a persistent source of discomfort in our lives, regardless of whether or not we meant it to be that way. It sneaks up on us in the middle of life's frenetic ups and downs, seizes our minds without prior notice, and sends us plunging into a state of profound tension and frustration.

However, it doesn't always have to be like this all the time. We can put an end to our habit of excessive thinking and instead go forward into a future that is filled with unbounded opportunities, clarity, and living in the here and now with a minimum of stress.

To be able to stop ourselves from dwelling on unnecessary thoughts that do not contribute to our progress, often known as "overthinking," we must first understand what the problem entails. In addition, it can manifest itself in a myriad of ways and is typically accompanied by pessimistic and hopeless thoughts.

It can be brought on by a variety of factors, such as a fear of confrontation or anxiety about the future, and you can readily recognize that you are overthinking if you are mentally weary, unable to focus, and possibly even losing sleep as a result. We are all aware that excessive pondering comes with a host of negative repercussions.

It may interfere with your ability to interact socially, prevent you from performing the duties assigned to you, cause anxiety and other issues related to mental health, and even disrupt the chemical equilibrium in your brain. As a result, we need to determine whether or not we have a problem with excessive thinking, admit it, and then put into practice methods that will help us break this pattern of behavior and rid ourselves of it for good.

Overthinking can also affect another element of our thoughts, namely our bad emotions, which should not be mistaken for negative thinking. Overthinking can bring on bad emotions in and of itself, just as negative emotions can bring on overthinking by themselves. However, we must recognize the unfavorable consequences that these feelings have on our thinking and that we only put into practice strategies to combat and manage negative feelings when they become disruptive to our lives.

In addition, anxiety is yet another element that is associated with overthinking. Overthinking has a similar kind of feedback looping interaction with unpleasant emotions as does negative feeling itself. We need to understand how stress can have adverse effects on us and contribute to excessive thinking so that we can effectively address these issues by practicing relaxation techniques.

In addition, the management of our time is important not just for our working life but also for our personal lives and our mental health. As a result, we ought to make the practice of prioritizing a habit, and in turn, we ought to set goals that are measurable, achievable, and time-efficient.

Furthermore, we ought to devise a daily or weekly schedule that will assist us in making the most of the 24 hours in a day, while still ensuring that we have sufficient time for our own requirements. Learning how to focus can help us combat the negative effects of overthinking and improve our ability to concentrate, both of which are beneficial to us.

Since overthinking and decision-making have a relationship that is similar to that of a loop, decision-making is another cognitive skill that can be negatively impacted by it. Overthinking can lead to poor decision-making, and vice versa. Poor decisions can also lead to overthinking. On the other hand, the process of decision-making can become significantly more effective with regular practice, a healthy dose of self-esteem, and many tactics designed to help overcome this challenge.

Last but not least, getting rid of unfavorable thoughts is a tried-and-true method for overcoming the effects of excessive pondering. Having negative ideas can feed overthinking even more, but there is a solution through the use of effective practices and approaches, just like there is a solution for everything else. Your thoughts don't have to be built on a foundation of negativity, and your life doesn't have to revolve around excessive levels of self-analysis and analysis paralysis.

Therefore, with what you have learned in this book, seize the day and make the conscious decision to break that annoying pattern of overthinking that you have developed. It won't happen overnight, so you need to take it one day at a time and keep in mind that patience is essential. However, if you are willing to put in the effort and put in the practice, you will be able to conquer the habit of overthinking in no time.

REFERENCES

Baker, M. (n.d). *The 9 different types of overthinking*. The Depression Project. https://thedepressionproject.com/blog/the-9-different-types-of-overthinking

Beard, C. (2020, April 26). *5 reasons why mental clarity is so important*. The Blissful Mind. https://theblissfulmind.com/mental-clarity/

Boyer, A. (2021, June 8). *9 signs you're overthinking something*. Introvert, Dear. https://introvertdear.com/news/9-signs-youre-overthinking-something/

Brennan, D. (2021, March 25). *What to know about stress and how it affects your mental health*. WebMD. https://www.webmd.com/balance/stress-management/stress-and-how-it-affects-your-mental-health

Chia, S. (2021, February 3). *Improve your focus and concentration: 15 ways to build your skills.* BetterUp. https://www.betterup.com/blog/15-ways-to-improve-your-focus-and-concentration-skills

Chukwuemeka, E. (2022, September 4). *Effect of overthinking on your mental, emotional and physical health.* BScholarly. https://bscholarly.com/effects-of-overthinking/

Davenport, B. (2022, October 19). *7 ways your choices have consequences.* Live Bold & Bloom. https://liveboldandbloom.com/10/self-awareness/choices-have-consequences

Davis, T. (n.d). *Priorities: Definition, list & tips.* Berkley Well-Being Institute. https://www.berkeleywellbeing.com/priorities.html

Effectivology. (n.d). *Why it's so hard to make decisions.* https://effectiviology.com/why-its-hard-to-make-decisions/

Fellow.app. (2021, December 13). *Goal prioritization: How to work effectively to meet goals.* https://fellow.app/blog/productivity/goal-prioritization-how-to-work-effectively-to-meet-goals/

Fillali, N. (2019, December 19). *The six pillars of self-esteem by Nathaniel Branden.* LinkedIn. https://www.linkedin.com/pulse/six-pillars-self-esteem-nathaniel-branden-naoufal-fillali/

Hull, M. (2022, May 26). *Harmful effects of stress*. The Recovery Village. https://www.therecoveryvillage.com/mental-health/stress/harmful-effects-of-stress/

Indeed Editorial Team. (2022, May 4). *Learn how to stop overthinking (Step and benefits)*. Indeed. https://in.indeed.com/career-advice/career-development/how-to-stop-overthinking

Johns Hopkins Medicine. (n.d.). *Recognizing and coping with negative emotions*. https://www.hopkinsmedicine.org/about/community_health/johns-hopkins-bayview/services/called_to_care/recognize_cope_with_negative_emotions.html

Johnson, B. (2011, April 1). *The 6 pillars of self-esteem*. Experience Life. https://experiencelife.lifetime.life/article/the-six-pillars-of-self-esteem/

Lamothe, C. (2022, June 7). *14 ways to stop overthinking*. Healthline. https://www.healthline.com/health/how-to-stop-overthinking#tally-up-wins

Marteka. (2019, July 15). *12 ways to recognize negative thoughts*. Benevolent health. https://benevolenthealth.co.uk/12-ways-to-recognise-negative-thoughts/

MasterClass. (2022, April 4). *How to make a schedule: 6 tips for scheduling*. https://www.masterclass.com/articles/how-to-make-a-schedule

MasterClass. (2022, May 10). *How to set goals: 5-step approach to setting goals.* https://www.masterclass.com/articles/setting-goals

Mayo Clinic Staff. (2022, April 28). *Relaxation techniques: Try these steps to reduce stress.* Mayo Clinic. https://www.mayoclinic.org/healthy-lifestyle/stress-management/in-depth/relaxation-technique/art-20045368

Mead, E. (2019, April 8). *What are negative emotions and how to control them?* PositivePsychology.com. https://positivepsychology.com/negative-emotions/

Metrinko, L. (2020, July 30). *7 dangerous effects of overthinking.* Psych2Go. https://psych2go.net/7-dangerous-effects-of-overthinking/

Mitiotti, A. (2015). The effects of chronic stress on health: New insights into the molecular mechanisms of brain–body communication. *Future Science OA, 1*(3). https://doi.org/10.4155/fso.15.21

NickWignall. (2021, February 17). *7 psychological reasons you overthink everything.* https://nickwignall.com/7-psychological-reasons-you-overthink-everything/

Oppong, T. (2019, July 25). *Stress is a byproduct of overthinking.* Ladders. https://www.theladders.com/career-advice/stress-is-a-byproduct-of-overthinking

Perera, K. (n.d). *Self esteem and self awareness*. More Self Esteem. https://more-selfesteem.com/more-self-esteem/building-self-esteem/what-is-self-esteem/self-awareness-and-self-esteem/

Rachert, J. (2022, July 6). *16 negative thought patterns in depression.* Heads Up Guys. https://headsupguys.org/common-negative-thought-patterns-in-depression/

Raypole, C. (2020, April 28). *How to become the boss of your emotions.* Healthline. https://www.healthline.com/health/how-to-control-your-emotions#get-some-space

Sandi, C., & Haller, J. (2015). Stress and the social brain: Behavioural effects and neurobiological mechanisms. *Nature Reviews Neuroscience, 16*(5), 290–304. https://doi.org/10.1038/nrn3918

Scott, E. (2022, May 24). *The toxic effects of negative self-talk.* Verywell Mind. https://www.verywellmind.com/negative-self-talk-and-how-it-affects-us-4161304

Silber, D. (2021, September 14). *The real effects of negative thinking.* Linkedin. https://www.linkedin.com/pulse/real-effects-negative-thinking-dr-debi-silber/

Susman, D. (2022, October 5). *How to stop overthinking.* Verywell Mind. https://www.verywellmind.com/how-to-know-when-youre-overthinking-5077069

Tarakovsky, M. (2015, July 8). *9 tips for identifying and living your priorities.* PsychCentral. https://psychcentral.com/blog/9-tips-for-identifying-and-living-your-priorities#5

Team Asana. (2022, July 27). *6 steps to create a daily schedule template.* Asana. https://asana.com/resources/daily-schedule-template

UMass Dartmouth. (n.d.). *Decision-making process.* https://www.umassd.edu/fycm/decision-making/process/

Usha, B. (2021, May 8). The benefits of concentration. *The Daily Guardian.* https://thedailyguardian.com/the-benefits-of-concentration/

Waters, S. (2021, August 5). *The path to self-acceptance, paved through daily practice.* BetterUp. https://www.betterup.com/blog/self-acceptance

Wayne, D. (2021, June 3). *Am I making the right decision?* Online Anxiety Therapy. https://www.millennialtherapy.com/anxiety-therapy-blog/am-i-making-the-right-decision

Wilding, M. (2022, June 6). *3 strategies to stop overthinking and make faster decisions.* LinkedIn. https://www.linkedin.com/business/learning/blog/career-success-tips/3-strategies-to-stop-overthinking-and-make-faster-decisons

Witmer, S. (2021, July 12). *What is overthinking and how do I stop overthinking everything?* GoodRX Health.

https://www.goodrx.com/well-being/healthy-mind/how-can-i-stop-overthinking-everything

Wright, A. (2022, May 19). *The benefits of relaxation and relaxation techniques to try*. Psych Central. https://psychcentral.com/lib/relaxation-make-time-and-take-time-for-self-care

www.ingramcontent.com/pod-product-compliance
Lightning Source LLC
Chambersburg PA
CBHW061159120626
46546CB00005B/2121